Independence Day

This patriotic quilt was made by Teresa and Amber Varnes. They chose to go purely patriotic in their colors of red, white, and blue and added some spark with yellow and green. It is made with 12" blocks set on-point with white lattice to blend into the background. The striped border finish adds just the right touch. This quilt will surely please the hero in your life.

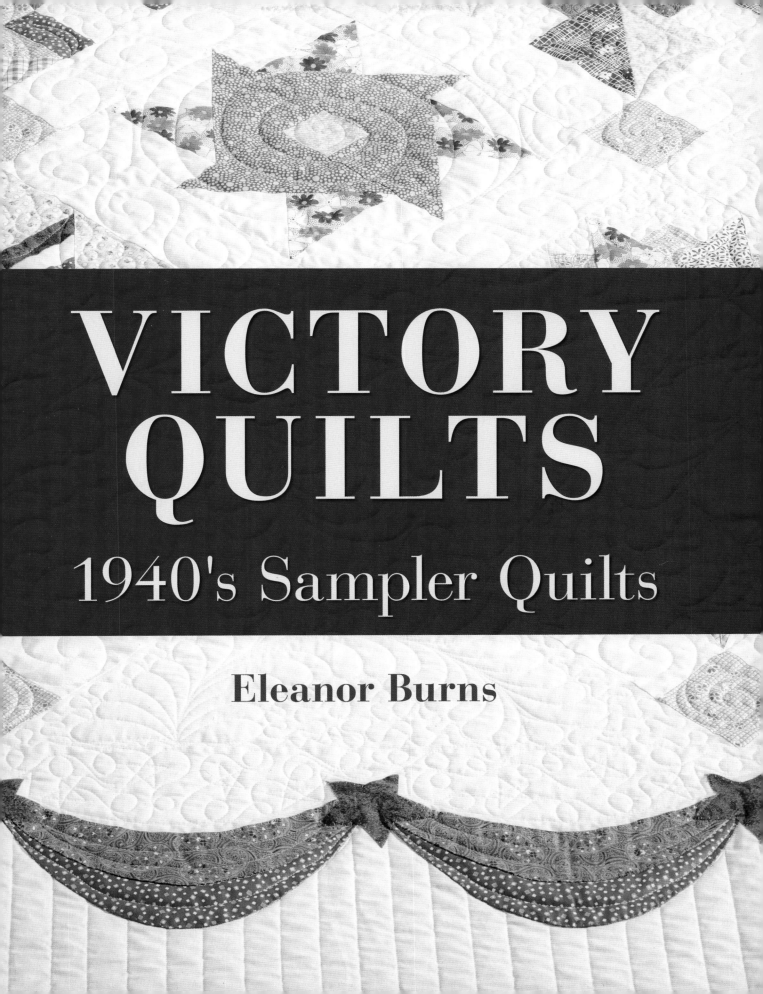

VICTORY QUILTS

1940's Sampler Quilts

Eleanor Burns

For Father, Erwin J. Knoechel,

*and all men and women who bravely
serve our country*

First Edition
April, 2008
Published by Quilt in a Day®, Inc.
1955 Diamond Street, San Marcos, CA 92078
©2008 by Eleanor A. Burns Family Trust

ISBN 1-891776-23-1

Art Director: Merritt Voigtlander
Production Artists: Marie Harper, Ann Huisman

Table of Contents

Introduction

The United States citizens of the 1940's have been called the greatest generation on earth. They were united with a common cause of winning World War II, either serving in the war or keeping the home front in tact. Rosie the Riveter was the symbol of working woman as the men went off to war. There were scrap drives, rationing, Victory Gardens, and the baby boom. The twenty quilt blocks in *Victory Quilts* tell the story of the decade. The 1940's also begins the story of my family.

In 1940, high school sweethearts Erma Drushel and Erwin Knoechel were enjoying life with President Roosevelt in command. When they heard his brilliant, uplifting voice over the radio, they knew they would come out of the Depression in the little town of Zelienople, Pennsylvania.

Erma was only twenty years old hoping to marry twenty-one year old Erwin, but her mother disapproved. After all, he was a German, immigrating to America in 1929 when he was nine years old… and everyone knew about Hitler, the German leader!

Life changed when Japan bombed Pearl Harbor on December 7, 1941. Just a few weeks later, on December 25, 1941, Erwin and Erma eloped. They were certain Erwin would soon be drafted.

With Erwin in the Army, Erma delivered her first daughter in 1943. She was kept busy raising Kathy, rationing, working in her Victory Garden, growing and canning their food, and supporting the war effort by purchasing Savings Bonds.

I was a baby boomer, an early fire cracker, born on July 3, 1945. It was the perfect time for celebration between Victory in Europe (VE Day on May 8, 1945) and Victory in Japan (VJ Day on August 15, 1945). For years, my mother said when I was born, my little toes with a V shaped pad, were Victory Toes. Life was good! Father would be home soon after serving Intelligence in Germany!

The Government passed the GI Bill, which helped our family prosper. My father was able to start his own heating and air conditioning business. He moved his four young daughters, Kathy, Eleanor, Patty, and Judy, into a perfect little ranch home in 1949.

This was just the beginning of my standing up and being proud! Independence Day with a parade and fireworks in our small town was just the culmination of my July 3 birthday!

Starting with Memorial Day and ending after Labor Day, I love to dress my home in patriotic decorations - flags, swags, and plenty of red, white and blue! I hang many quilts that I have made, but I also love to decorate with antique quilts.

I recently added these two quilts to my collection that were obviously made for loved ones in the service. The USN quilt came with The Bluejackets' Manual, 1944, signed by Millard Clark, Co551, possibly the owner. It's beautifully hand quilted, and in excellent condition. The second one is a summer quilt with all pieces appliqued to the top. The border pieces are intricate, and a perfect accent.

I had fun dressing up as the original Rosie from Norman Rockwell's painting. She first appeared on the cover of the Saturday Evening Post on May 29, 1943. Even though I'm not as muscular as Rosie, I was happy eating a great sandwich with my rivet gun resting across my lap, proud as can be. So have fun! Be happy!

Enjoy making a patriotic Victory Quilt for a hero in your life!

Eleanor Burns

Planning Your Quilt

On Point Setting for 18 Blocks with Swags and Stars

Yardage is given for On Point and Straight Settings in both 12" and 6" blocks. Each setting can be made in two sizes from a different number of blocks. Border treatments include a Swag Border, Ribbon Border, or Plain Border.

Decide where you will display or use your quilt to determine the size needed.

Eighteen 12" Blocks
88" x 108"
Pieced by Teresa Varnes
Quilted by Cindee Ferris

Eighteen 6" Blocks
50" x 60"
Pieced by Eleanor Burns
Quilted by Carol Selepec

On Point Setting for 18 Blocks with Swags and Stars

	12" Blocks 88" x 108"	6" Blocks 50" x 60"
Background	7 yds	2½ yds
Lattice	(16) 3½" strips cut into (48) 3½" x size of block	(8) 2" strips cut into (48) 2" x size of block
Side Triangles (See illustration below.) Side Triangles Lattice	(3) 22½" strips cut each into (1) 22½" square (6) 3½" x size of block	(1) 12" strip cut into (3) 12" squares
Corner Triangles	(1) 14" strip cut into (2) 14" squares	(2) 7½" squares
Border	(9) 10½" strips	(5) 9" strips
Cornerstones	**⅓ yd**	**¼ yd**
	(3) 3½" strips cut into (31) 3½" squares	(2) 2" strips cut into (31) 2" squares
Binding	**1 yd**	**¾ yd**
	(10) 3" strips	(6) 3" strips
Backing	9 yds 45" fabric or 3 yds 108" fabric	3½ yds 45" fabric or 1¾ yds 96" fabric
Batting	106" x 116"	58" x 68"

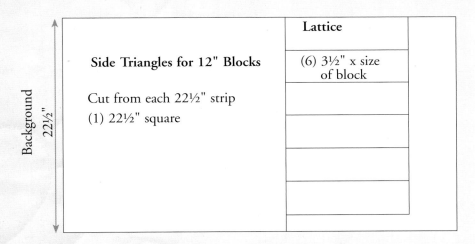

Background 22½"

Side Triangles for 12" Blocks

Cut from each 22½" strip
(1) 22½" square

Lattice

(6) 3½" x size of block

Swags and Stars

	12" Blocks	6" Blocks
Medium Blue	**1 yd**	**⅔ yd**
Top Swag and Corners	(3) 10½" strips cut into (6) 10½" x 21"	(2) 10½" strips cut into (3) 10½" x 21"
Dark Red	**1⅓ yds**	**⅔ yd**
Bottom Swag and Corners	(4) 10½" strips cut into (8) 10½" x 21"	(2) 10½" strips cut into (4) 10½" x 21"
Non-woven Fusible Interfacing	4¼ yds	2½ yds
	(14) 10½" x 21" strips	(7) 10½" x 21" strips
Stars	**½ yd**	**½ yd**
	32 Small Stars	14 Small Stars and 4 Large Stars
Paper Backed Fusible Web	⅔ yd	⅔ yd

On Point Setting for 13 Blocks with Swags and Stars

This quilt features a 7½" wide striped border from Victory Garden fabric line. To figure stripe yardage, measure the longest side of quilt top. Add ½ yd to that measurement to allow for mitering stripe.

Thirteen 12" Blocks
80" x 80"
Pieced by Amber and Teresa Varnes, and Eleanor Burns
Quilted by Cindee Ferris

Thirteen 6" Blocks
50" x 50"
Pieced by Amber and Teresa Varnes
Quilted by Amie Potter

On Point Setting for 13 Blocks with Swags and Stars

	12" Blocks 88" x 88"	6" Blocks 50" x 50"
Background	5½ yds	2¼ yds
Lattice	(12) 3½" strips cut into (36) 3½" x size of block	(6) 2" strips cut into (36) 2" x size of block

Side Triangles (See illustration below.)
   Side Triangles
   Lattice
	(2) 22½" strips cut each into
	(1) 22½" square
	(6) 3½" x size of block
		(1) 12" strip cut into
		(2) 12" squares

Corner Triangles	(1) 14" strip cut into (2) 14" squares	(2) 7½" squares
Border	(8) 10½" strips	(5) 9" strips
Cornerstones	⅓ yd	¼ yd
	(3) 3½" strips cut into (24) 3½" squares	(2) 2" strips cut into (24) 2" squares
Binding	1 yd	¾ yd
	(9) 3" strips	(6) 3" strips
Backing	8 yds 45" fabric or 3 yds 96" fabric	3½ yds 45" fabric or 1¾ yds 96" fabric
Batting	96" x 96"	58" x 58"

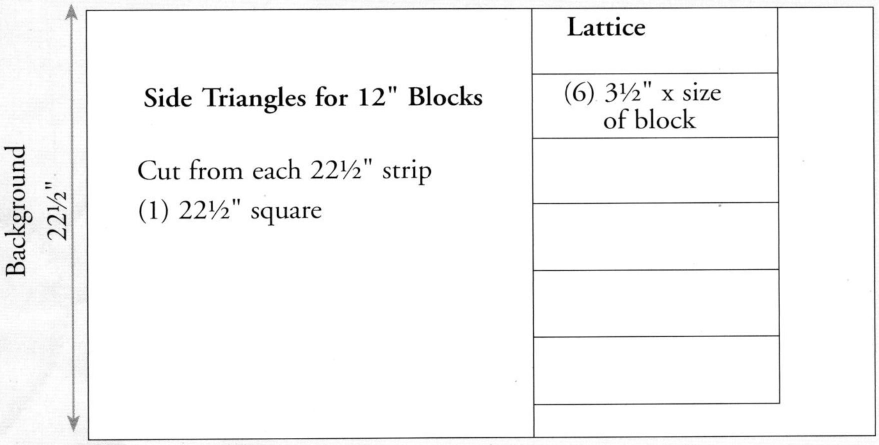

```
Side Triangles for 12" Blocks          Lattice

Cut from each 22½" strip               (6) 3½" x size
(1) 22½" square                             of block

Background 22½"
```

Swags and Stars		
Medium Blue	1 yd	⅔ yd
Top Swag	(3) 10½" strips cut into (4) 10½" x 21" for 24 Swags	(2) 10½" strips cut into (3) 10½" x 21" for 16 Swags
Top Corners	(2) 10½" x 21" for 4 Corners	_____
Red	1¼ yds	⅔ yd
Bottom Swag	(4) 10½" strips cut into (5) 10½" x 21" for 24 Swags	(2) 10½" strips cut into (4) 10½" x 21" for 16 Swags
Bottom Corners	(2) 10½" x 21" for 4 Corners	_____
Non-woven Fusible Interfacing	4 yds	2½ yds
Swags and Corners	(13) 10½" x 21" strips	(7) 10½" x 21" strips
Stars	½ yd	½ yd
	28 small Stars	12 small Stars and 4 large Stars
Paper Backed Fusible Web	⅔ yd	⅔ yd

Straight Setting for 20 Blocks with Ribbon Border

This quilt features plain Borders. To figure plain Border yardage, find the number and width of strips needed in the yardage chart. Multiply these two numbers to figure amount of yardage needed per Border.

Reduce the amount of Border yardage from the original yardage.

Twenty 12" Blocks
88" x 102"
Pieced by Sally Murray
Quilted by Janna Mitchell

Twenty 6" Blocks
50" x 56"
3" Finished Size Ribbon Border
Pieced by Patricia Knoechel
Quilted by Amie Potter

Straight Setting for 20 Blocks with Ribbon Border

	12" Blocks 96" x 112"	6" Blocks 51" x 57"
Background	5¾ yds	1⅝ yds
Lattice	(17) 3½" strips cut into (49) 3½" x size of block	(9) 2" strips cut into (49) 2" x size of block
First Border	(4) 3" strips for Sides (4) 3½" strips for Top and Bottom	(2) 2½" strips for Sides (2) 2" strips for Top and Bottom
Second Border	(11) 10½" strips	(5) 5" strips
Cornerstones	⅓ yd	¼ yd
	(3) 3½" strips cut into (30) 3½" squares	(2) 2" strips cut into (30) 2" squares
Binding	**1 yd**	**¾ yd**
	(11) 3" strips	(6) 3" strips
Backing	9 yds 45" fabric or 3¼ yds 108" fabric	3¼ yds 45" fabric or 1⅔ yds 108" fabric
Batting	104" x 120"	60" x 66"

Ribbon Border

	4" Finished Size	3" Finished Size
	(76) Little and Large Points	(52) Little and Large Points
	(4) Corners	(4) Corners
Background	⅝ yd	⅓ yd
Little Points	(3) 5½" strips cut into (19) 5½" squares	(2) 4½" strips cut into (13) 4½" squares
Corners	(2) 5" squares	(2) 4" squares
Red	⅝ yd	⅓ yd
Little Points	(3) 5½" strips cut into (19) 5½" squares	(2) 4½" strips cut into (13) 4½" squares
Corners	(2) 5" squares	(2) 4" squares
Dark Blue	¾ yd	⅜ yd
Large Points	(5) 5" strips cut into (38) 5" squares	(3) 4" strips cut into (26) 4" squares

Straight Setting for 12 Blocks with Ribbon Border

Twelve 12" Blocks
67" x 83"
4" Finished Size Ribbon Border
Pieced and Quilted by Anne Tracy

Twelve 6" Blocks
44" x 50"
3" Finished Size Ribbon Border
Pieced by Sue Bouchard
Quilted by Cindee Ferris

Straight Setting for 12 Blocks and Ribbon Border

	12" Blocks 66" x 82"	6" Blocks 45" x 51"
Background	2¾ yds	1½ yds

Lattice	(11) 2½" strips cut into
	    (31) 2½" x size of block
		(6) 2" strips cut into
		    (31) 2" x size of block

First Border	(3) 2⅝" strips for Sides (3) 3⅝" strips for Top and Bottom	(2) 3½" strips for Sides (2) 2¾" strips for Top and Bottom
Second Border	(7) 6" strips	(4) 5" strips
Cornerstones	¼ yd	⅛ yd

	(2) 2½" strips cut into
	    (20) 2½" squares
		(1) 2" strip cut into
		    (20) 2" squares

Binding	⅔ yd	½ yd
	(7) 3" strips	(5) 3" strips
Backing	5 yds 45" fabric or 2¼ yds 96" fabric	3 yds 45" fabric or 2 yds 96" fabric
Batting	76" x 90"	52" x 58"

	4" Finished Size	3" Finished Size
	(56) Little and Large Points	(44) Little and Large Points
	(4) Corners	(4) Corners
Background	⅔ yd	⅓ yd

Little Points	(2) 5½" strips cut into
	    (14) 5½" squares
		(2) 4½" strips cut into
		    (11) 4½" squares

Corners	(2) 5" squares	(2) 4" squares
Red	⅔ yd	⅓ yd

Little Points	(2) 5½" strips cut into
	    (14) 5½" squares
		(2) 4½" strips cut into
		    (11) 4½" squares

Corners	(2) 5" squares	(2) 4" squares
Dark Blue	⅔ yd	½ yd

Large Points	(4) 5" strips cut into
	    (28) 5" squares
		(3) 4" strips cut into
		    (22) 4" squares

Ribbon Border

Selecting Your Block Fabrics

In the early 1940's, fabrics were scarce, with cotton the most popular and affordable. Influenced by current events, most colors were vibrant and patriotic in red, white, and blue. They were named flag red, glory blue, cadet blue, aircorps blue, navy, and army tan. Military designs as sailors, stars, and stripes were popular motifs.

To have an authentic looking Victory Quilt, select fabrics recreating the 1940's. The numbers underneath these patriotic floral swatches are from **The Victory Garden** fabric line by Eleanor Burns for Benartex.

A fat quarter measures 18" x 20"
A fat eighth measures 9" x 20"

	12" Blocks	**6" Blocks**
Background	2 yds of one Background or 2 yds total of multiple fabrics	1 yd of one Background or 1 yd total of multiple fabrics

3927-77   3926-77   3924-77

Large Scale Floral	Two fat quarters	Two fat eighths

3923-55   3923-10

Yellow	Three fat quarters	Three fat eighths

3926-33   3924-33   3929-33

Deep Mint Green	Two fat quarters	Two fat eighths

3929-44   3926-44

Flag Red to Rose	Four fat quarters	Four fat eighths

3926-10   3924-10   3929-10   3931-10

Cadet Blue/Navy	Six fat quarters	Six fat eighths

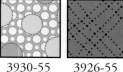

3930-55   3926-55   3929-55   3924-55   3931-55   3927-58

Planning Your Blocks

Select your blocks based on number needed, skill level, and technique.

There are twenty different blocks to choose from in skill levels from easy to advanced. All blocks are traditional in style and were selected from Barbara Brackman's *Encyclopedia of Pieced Quilt Patterns* to tell the story of the Forties. Original designers and the years they were published are included.

If you are a beginner, select 12" blocks marked with one star to improve your skills. Continue your skill building with two star intermediate and three star advanced blocks. Less than perfect blocks or extra blocks can be sewn into the backing. If you are an experienced quilter looking for a challenge, select 6" blocks in all skill levels.

Skill Level	*Easy* ★	*Intermediate* ★ ★	*Advanced* ★ ★ ★

Strip Piecing

 Comfort Quilt
page 52
★

Triangle Pieced Squares
Using 6½" Triangle Square Up Ruler

 Mr. Roosevelt's Necktie
page 26
★

 Contrary Wife
page 90
★

 Broken Sugar Bowl
page 104
★

 Propeller
page 144
★

Quarter Triangle Pieced Squares

 Silent Star
page 34
★

Partial Seaming

 Radio Windmill
page 72
★

 Hope of Hartford
page 162
★

Mini Geese Rulers

 1941 Nine-Patch
page 60
★ ★

 Army Star
page 132
★ ★

Applique

 Fala
page 42
★

 Star Spangled Banner
page 96
★

 Stars and Stripes
page 122
★

Two Patches at Same Time

 Brave World
page 200
★

Template Piecing

 Sky Rocket
page 78
★ ★ ★

 Signal Lights
page 112
★ ★ ★

 Airplane
page 150
★ ★

 Victory Block
page 182
★ ★ ★

Y Seams

 Liberty Star
page 172
★ ★ ★

 Bride's Bouquet
page 190
★ ★ ★

Supplies

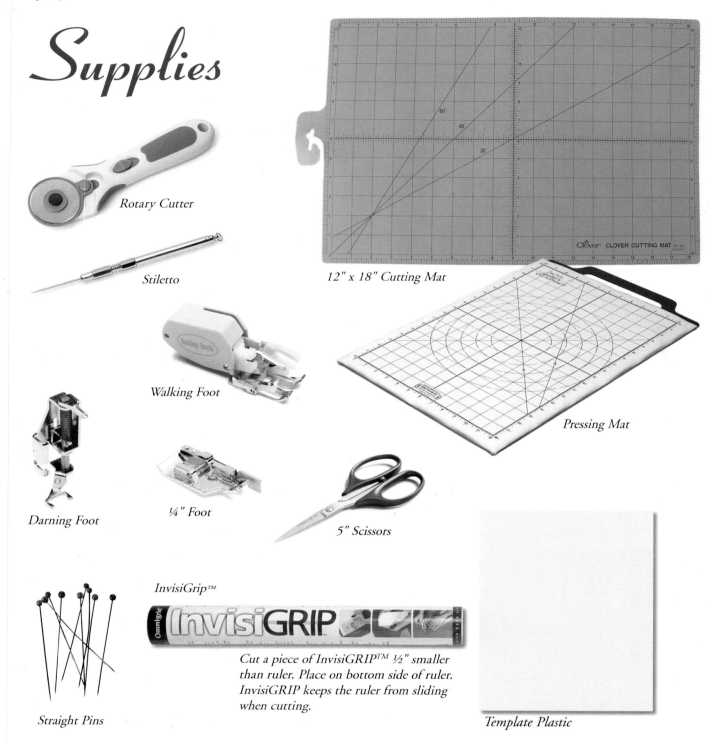

Rotary Cutter

Stiletto

12" x 18" Cutting Mat

Walking Foot

Pressing Mat

Darning Foot

¼" Foot

5" Scissors

InvisiGrip™

InvisiGRIP

Cut a piece of InvisiGRIP™ ½" smaller than ruler. Place on bottom side of ruler. InvisiGRIP keeps the ruler from sliding when cutting.

Straight Pins

Template Plastic

Applique Tools for Fala

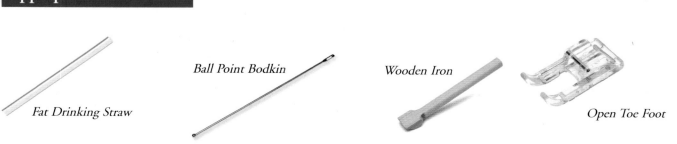

Fat Drinking Straw

Ball Point Bodkin

Wooden Iron

Open Toe Foot

Rulers

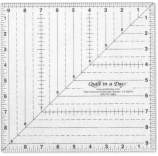

9½" Square Up Ruler

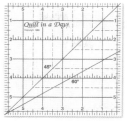

6" Square Up Ruler

6½" Triangle Square Up Ruler

Mini Geese Ruler One

Mini Geese Ruler Two

Fussy Cut Rulers in Four Sizes: 6½", 4½", 3½, and 2½"

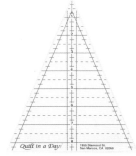

Kaleidoscope Ruler

6" x 24" Ruler

4" x 14" Ruler

THE SIX BY TWELVE

6" x 12" Ruler

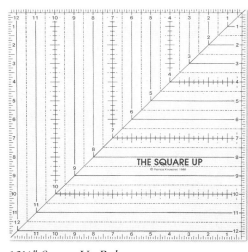

THE SQUARE UP

12½" Square Up Ruler for 12½" Blocks

Quilting Supplies

Pins with Pin Covers

Kwik Klip

Clamps

Cutting Your Quilt

Each block is shown in color with suggested fabric to use for each piece, plus the size to cut for both 12" and 6" finished blocks.

You can individually cut each block before you sew it, or you can assembly-line cut all blocks before you begin sewing. Assembly-line cutting Background is the best use of time and fabric. See pages 20-21. Once cutting is completed, each block takes approximately one hour or less.

Cutting Strips for Individual Blocks

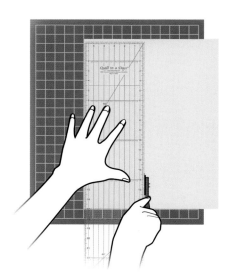

1. Select designated fabric according to individual chart, and press.

2. Select ruler slightly longer than designated size. Best rulers to use for strips are the 4" x 14", 6" x 24", and 6" x 12" rulers. Straighten left edge.

3. Move ruler over until ruler lines are at newly cut edge. Carefully and accurately line up and cut strips at measurements given.

   Strips for Liberty Star (page 172) and Star Spangled Banner (page 96) should be cut first because they need the full width of the fabric.

Cutting Squares and Rectangles

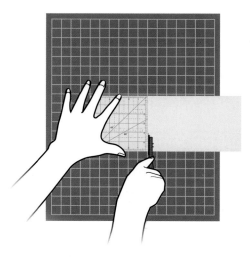

1. Select ruler slightly larger than designated size. Best rulers to use for cutting squares and rectangles are the 6" x 12", 6", 9½", and 12½" Square Up rulers. Place ruler on left corner of fabric, lining up ruler with grain of fabric.

2. Rotary cut pieces on right side of ruler, and across top, slightly larger than designated size.

3. Turn piece and cut to exact size.

Cut first measurement the height of the strip, and second measurement the length.

Fussy Cuts

A fussy cut is a selected image, such as a flower, centered on your patch. With a Fussy Cut Ruler™, you can cut the identical image repeatedly with ease.

There are four sizes of Fussy Cut Rulers™ available: 2½", 3½", 4½" and 6½". Perfect places for Fussy Cuts are the center or four corners of your block, or Cornerstones.

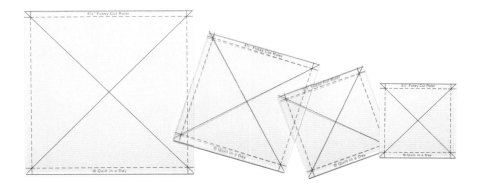

How to Make a Fussy Cut

1. To keep ruler from slipping while cutting, cut InvisiGRIP™ ½" smaller than ruler and press on bottom side.

2. Find image on fabric that fits within size needed.

3. Place ruler on top of image, with center of X on center of image. The dashed lines indicate the seam lines. Shift ruler so image fits within seam lines.

4. If it's critical that each image be identical, place a piece of InvisiGRIP™ on top side of Fussy Cut Ruler. Trace outline of fussy cut on the top piece with a permanent marking pen. Remove top InvisiGRIP™ after cutting all squares.

5. Cut around ruler with rotary cutter. To keep the ruler centered, place fabric and ruler on Brooklyn Revolver™ or Olfa® Rotating Mat, and rotate mat as you cut.

6. To make your own template, cut appropriate size square from template plastic. Draw an X and ¼" seam lines. Place on image, draw around template, and cut out with rotary cutter and ruler.

Assembly-line Cutting Background for Twenty Blocks

If you are making fewer blocks, eliminate cutting those pieces.

1. Label a plastic quart size bag with name of each block.

2. Cut first Background strip at indicated width, selvage to selvage, with 6" x 24" ruler.

3. Turn strip and straighten left edge. Cut strip into indicated sizes of squares and rectangles. **Some strips are cut narrower than original width for best use of fabric.**

4. Label each piece if desired and put into appropriate block's bag.

If you are making fewer blocks, eliminate cutting those pieces.
Some strips are cut narrower than original width for best use of fabric.

Assembly-line Cutting Background for Twenty 12" Blocks — 2 yds

☐ (1) 12½" strip cut into

Fala	(1) 12½" square
Victory	(1) 9¾" x 20"
Hope of Hartford	(1) 6½" square

☐ (1) 5½" strip cut into

Silent Star	(2) 5½" squares
1941 Nine-Patch	(1) 5½" square
Army Star	(1) 3½" x 15"

☐ (1) 5" strip cut into

Silent Star	(1) 5" x 10"
Contrary Wife	(1) 5" x 10"
Brave World	(1) 4½" x 15"

☐ (1) 4½" strip cut into

| 1941 Nine-Patch | (4) 4½" squares |
| Broken Sugar Bowl | (2) 4½" squares |

☐ (1) 4⅛" strip cut into

| Airplane | (2) 4⅛" x 5¼" |
| Mr. Roosevelt's Necktie | (2) 4" squares |

☐ (1) 3½" strip cut into

| Mr. Roosevelt's Necktie | (8) 3½" squares |
| Bride's Bouquet | (1) 3¼" x 10¾" |

☐ (1) 3¼" strip cut into

Comfort Quilt	(4) 3¼" squares
Signal Light	(2) 3¼" x 7¾"
Bride's Bouquet	(1) 3¼" x 10¾"

☐ (2) 3" strips cut into

Airplane	(2) 3" x 7½"
Victory	(4) 3" x 6"
Propeller	(1) 2⅞" x 13"
Propeller	(1) 2⅞" square

☐ (3) 2¾" strips cut into

Bride's Bouquet	(1) 2¾" x 22"
Bride's Bouquet	(1) 2¾" x 11"
Sky Rocket	(8) 2¾" x 8¼"
Airplane	(4) 2¾" x 3"

☐ (1) 2½" strip cut into

Broken Sugar Bowl	(1) 2½" x 6"
Hope of Hartford	(4) 2½" x 5½"
Airplane	(1) 2" x 3"
Airplane	(2) 1¾" squares
Airplane	(1) 1¾" x 3"

☐ (1) 1⅞" strip cut into

| Star Spangled Banner | (1) 1⅞" x 20" |
| Stars and Stripes | (2) 1¾" x 10" |

| Liberty Star | **☐ (1) 1⅜" strip** |

If you are making fewer blocks, eliminate cutting those pieces.
Some strips are cut narrower than original width for best use of fabric.

Assembly-line Cutting Twenty 6" Blocks — 1 yd

☐ **(1) 6½" strip cut into**

Fala	(1) 6½" square
Victory	(1) 5½" x 11"
Hope of Hartford	(1) 3¾" square

☐ **(1) 3½" strip cut into**

Silent Star	(2) 3½" squares
1941 Nine-Patch	(1) 3½" square
Silent Star	(1) 3" x 6"
Contrary Wife	(1) 3" x 6"
Brave World	(1) 3" x 9"

☐ **(1) 2½" strip cut into**

Mr. Roosevelt's Necktie	(2) 2½" squares
1941 Nine-Patch	(4) 2½" squares
Broken Sugar Bowl	(2) 2½" squares
Airplane	(2) 2½" x 3½"

☐ **(1) 2¼" strip cut into**

Victory	(4) 2¼" x 4¼"
Comfort Quilt	(4) 1⅞" squares

☐ **(2) 2" strips cut into**

Mr. Roosevelt's Necktie	(8) 2" squares
Signal Lights	(2) 2" x 4¾"
Army Star	(1) 2" x 9"
Bride's Bouquet	(2) 2" x 6⅛"

☐ **(3) 1¾" strips cut into**

Sky Rocket	(8) 1¾" x 5"
Propeller	(1) 1¾" square
Propeller	(1) 1¾" x 8"
Airplane	(4) 1¾" squares
Airplane	(2) 1¾" x 4⅛"
Hope of Hartford	(4) 1¾" x 2⅞"
Bride's Bouquet	(1) 1¾" x 8"
Bride's Bouquet	(1) 1¾" x 14"

☐ **(1) 1½" strip cut into**

Broken Sugar Bowl	(1) 1½" x 4"
Airplane	(1) 1¼" x 1¾"
Star Spangled Banner	(1) 1⅛" x 11"
Stars and Stripes	(2) 1⅛" x 6"
Airplane	(2) 1⅛" squares
Airplane	(1) 1⅛" x 1¾"

☐ **(1) 1" strip cut into**

Liberty Star	(2) 1" x 13"

Techniques

¼" Seam Allowance Test

Use a consistent ¼" seam allowance throughout construction of quilt. If necessary, adjust needle position, change presser foot, or feed fabric under the presser foot to achieve ¼". **Complete the ¼" seam allowance test before starting.**

1. Cut (3) 1½" x 6" pieces.

2. Set machine at 15 stitches per inch, or 2.0 on computerized machines.

3. Sew three strips together lengthwise with what you **think** is a ¼" seam.

4. Press seams in one direction. Make sure no folds occur at seam.

5. Place sewn sample under a ruler and measure its width. **It should measure exactly 3½".** If sample measures smaller than 3½", seam is too large. If sample measures larger than 3½", seam is too small. Adjust seam and repeat if necessary.

Pressing

Individual instructions usually say which fabric should be on top, and which fabric seams should be pressed toward.

1. Place on pressing mat, with fabric on top that seam is to be pressed toward. Set seam by pressing stitches.

2. Open and press against seam.

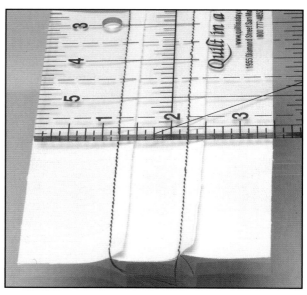

It is important to know how many needle positions are on your sewing machine. Moving your needle one position to the right of center while using a ¼" foot may be better than sewing in center needle position. A reduction of one thread width compensates for width gained in the fold of a seam.

For instance, when a computerized machine automatically sets itself at 3.5 for center, moving the needle one position to the right at 4.0 may give you the desired finished size of block.

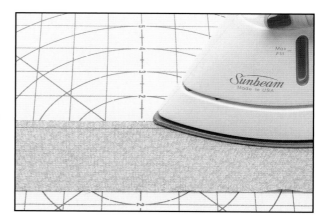

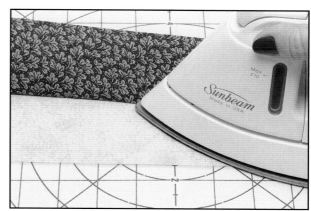

Unsewing Center Seams

To make seams lie flat, use this technique for these blocks:

Blocks with Four-Patch Center from wrong side
Liberty Star
Bride's Bouquet
Silent Star

Blocks with Pinwheel Center from wrong side
Radio Windmill
Brave World
Victory Block

1. At the center seam, cut the first stitch with scissors.

2. Remove the two or three vertical stitches at the center with stiletto or seam ripper.

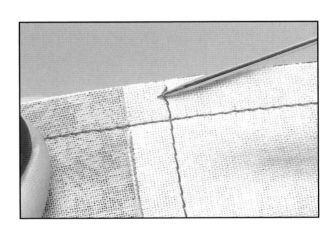

3. Turn block over, and repeat removing vertical stitches at center.

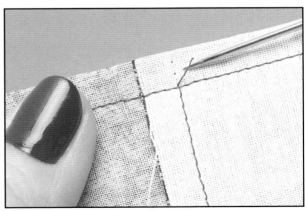

4. Open the center seams and push down flat to form a tiny four-patch or pinwheel.

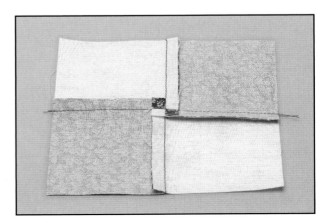

Squaring Up Triangle Pieced Squares

Triangle Pieced Squares are oversized and need to be trimmed. This technique is called "squaring up". Use the Quilt in a Day 6½" Triangle Square Up Ruler to trim these blocks:

Mr. Roosevelt's Necktie	**Contrary Wife**	**Army Star**
Broken Sugar Bowl	**Silent Star**	**Propeller**

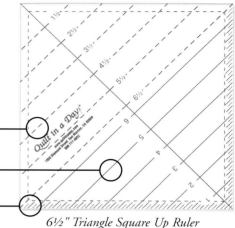

One half of the ruler is used for trimming patches with ½" measurements from 1½" to 6½". These are marked with red dashed lines.

The second half is used for trimming patches with whole measurements from 1" to 6" marked in solid green lines. Additional measurements are marked in ¼" or ⅛" increments. Red marks are ¼" lines, and shorter green lines are ⅛" lines.

6½" Triangle Square Up Ruler

1. Stack closed triangles lighter side up.

2. Look for uneven edges. Freshly cut edges don't need to be trimmed.

3. Place Invisigrip™ on bottom side of ruler so ruler does not slide while trimming.

4. Lay one test triangle on the cutting mat.

5. Each block indicates what size to square the patch to. **Lay the ruler's indicated square up line on top edge of stitching line to compensate for fold.**

6. Line up top edge of ruler with triangle. Hold ruler firmly.

7. Trim right side of triangle, pushing rotary cutter toward the point to avoid damaging the ruler's corner.

The example shows squaring the triangle to 2½". The 2½" line on the ruler is above the stitching.

8. Turn patch. Trim tips with rotary cutter and ruler. From stitching, trim a 45° angle.

9. Tips can also be trimmed with scissors, using a 60° angle to assure that seam allowance does not show after triangle is pressed open.

    You can also trim tips after pieced square is pressed open.

10. Lay trimmed triangle on pressing mat, triangle side up. Lift corner and press toward seam with tip of iron, pushing seams to triangle side. Press carefully so pieces do not distort.

11. Measure with 6" Square Up ruler to see if it is desired size. If not correct size, adjust placement of 6½" Triangle Square Up. Place line on stitching if square is too large. If square is too small, move ruler line slightly above stitching line.

Mr. Roosevelt's Necktie

Americans were living in very tough times with rampant unemployment, bank closures, and the Great Depression. There was war and unrest in Europe. People were afraid and needed a leader who could give hope and make changes. Franklin Delano Roosevelt, FDR as he was known, was elected President of the United States in 1932 and served for 12 years. In his inauguration address, he stated those famous words "We have nothing to fear but fear itself." FDR was an optimist, offering hope to millions of Americans who were without hope. His extreme self-confidence gave faith to the American people that better times were ahead.

FDR was a president of the people and endeared himself with fireside chats delivered over the radio. The casual and relaxed setting of these radio talks centered on issues of public concern and made Americans feel as if the president was speaking directly to them. This is an excerpt from his Fireside Chat on October 12, 1942: This whole nation of one hundred and thirty million free men, women and children is becoming one great fighting force. Some of us are soldiers or sailors, some of us are civilians. Some of us are fighting the war in airplanes five miles above the continent of Europe or the islands of the Pacific and some of us are fighting it in mines deep down in the earth of Pennsylvania or Montana. A few of us are decorated with medals for heroic achievement, but all of us can have that deep and permanent inner satisfaction that comes from doing the best we know how each of us playing an honorable part in the great struggle to save our democratic civilization.

OUR PRESIDENT
FRANKLIN D.
ROOSEVELT

Skill Level ★

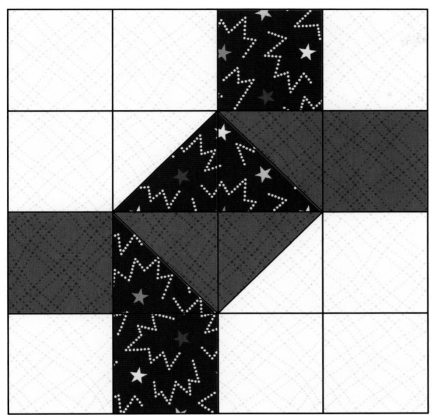

Supplies

12" Block
6½" Triangle Square Up Ruler
12½" Square Up Ruler

6" Block
6½" Triangle Square Up Ruler
9½" Square Up Ruler

	12" Finished Block	6" Finished Block
Background		
Knot	(2) 4" squares	(2) 2½" squares
Corners	(1) 3½" x 29" strip cut into	(1) 2" x 17" strip cut into
	(8) 3½" squares	(8) 2" squares
Medium		
Knot	(2) 4" squares	(2) 2½" squares
String	(2) 3½" squares	(2) 2" squares
Dark		
Knot	(2) 4" squares	(2) 2½" squares
String	(2) 3½" squares	(2) 2" squares

Making Knot Pieced Squares

1. Place three sets of squares right sides together. Draw diagonal lines.

12" Finished Block	6" Finished Block
4" squares	2½" squares

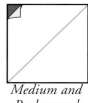

Dark and Medium   *Dark and Background*   *Medium and Background*

2. Assembly-line sew ¼" from both sides of diagonal line.

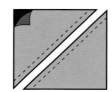
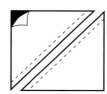
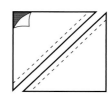

3. With rotary cutter and ruler, cut squares in half on diagonal line.

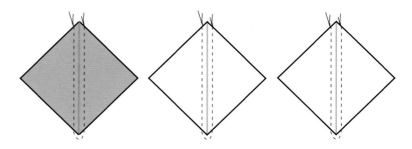

4. Square patches with 6½" Triangle Square Up Ruler.

12" Finished Block	6" Finished Block
3½" squares	2" squares

12" Block

Place **3½" red dashed line** on 6½" Triangle Square Up Ruler **above stitching line to compensate for fold.** Center ruler on patch. Trim two sides.

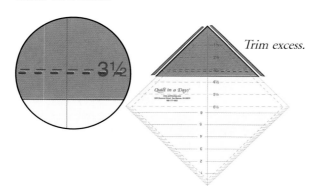

Trim excess.

6" Block

Place **2" green solid line** on 6½" Triangle Square Up Ruler **above stitching line to compensate for fold.** Center ruler on patch. Trim two sides.

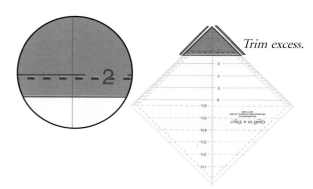

Trim excess.

5. Set seam. Open patch, and press.

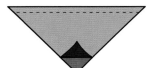 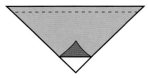

Press one seam toward medium. Press one seam toward dark.

Press seams toward dark.   *Press seams toward medium.*

6. Trim tips.

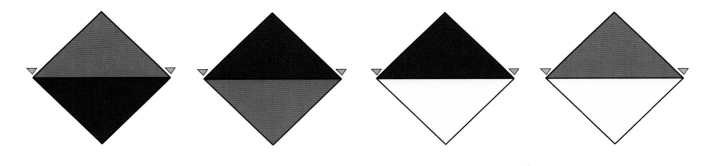

You end up with this many patches:

Two Medium/Dark

Two Background/ Dark One is extra.

Two Background/ Medium One is extra.

Sewing Block Together

1. Lay out Knot with squares.

12" Finished Block	6" Finished Block
3½" squares	2" squares

2. Flip second vertical row right sides together to first vertical row.

3. Assembly line sew. Do not clip connecting threads. Open.

4. Flip third vertical row right sides together to second vertical row.

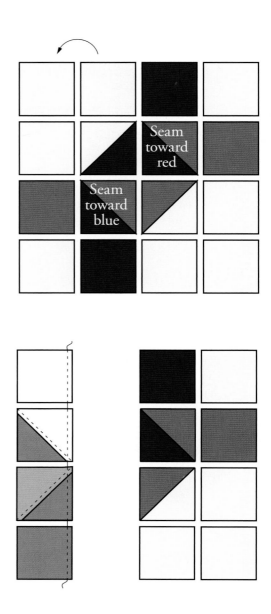

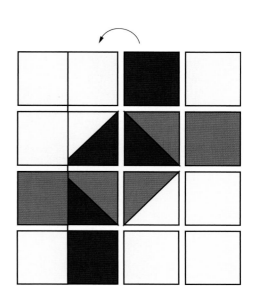

5. Lock diagonal seams on second and third patches.

6. Assembly line sew. Do not clip connecting threads. Open.

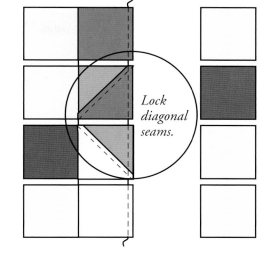

Lock diagonal seams.

7. Flip fourth vertical row right sides together to third vertical row.

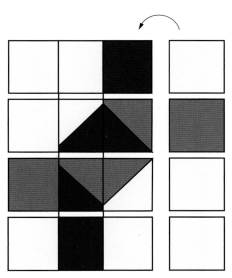

8. Assembly line sew. Do not clip connecting threads. Open.

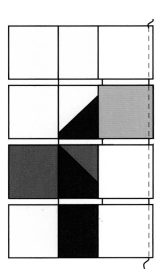

9. Turn block one quarter turn to the left.

10. Flip fourth vertical row right sides together to third vertical row.

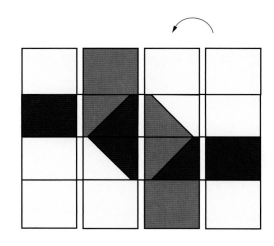

11. Lock seams together. Push top seam up, and underneath seam down.

12. Assembly line sew. Open.

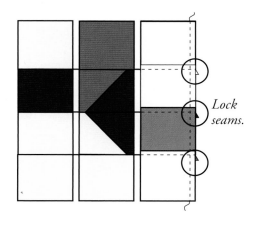

Lock seams.

13. Flip third vertical row right sides together to second vertical row.

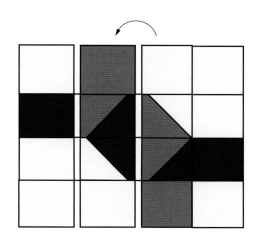

14. Push top seam down, and underneath seam up. Lock seams. Assembly line sew. Open.

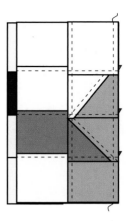

15. Flip second row right sides together to first vertical row.

16. Push top seam up, and underneath seam down. Lock seams. Assembly line sew. Open.

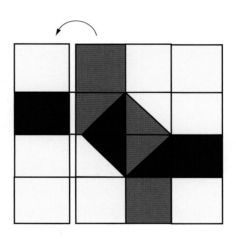

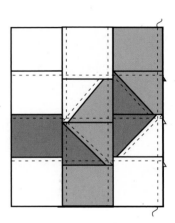

17. Press seams away from center.

18. Measure and record in box.

12" Finished Block	6" Finished Block

12½ " is ideal size   6½ " is ideal size
It is important that all blocks be one consistent size.

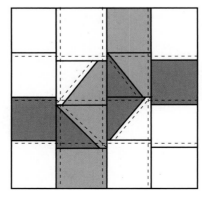

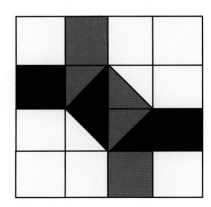

Silent Star

Adolph Hitler, head of the Nazi party, had ruled Germany since 1933. In March 1938, Hitler's troops crossed the Austrian border and took over Austria. In 1939, they took over Czechoslovakia and Poland. After Hitler ignored warnings to withdraw his troops, Great Britain and France declared war on Germany, officially starting World War II.

America was determined to stay out of the fighting! They would remain silent! World War I had left most Americans disillusioned about war. In addition, the United States was still recovering from the depression, which had left millions of Americans struggling to find jobs, food, and housing.

Because the United States was not directly involved in the war, the entire burden of the fighting fell on other nations, mostly Great Britain. Fortunately, Winston Churchill, Prime Minister of Great Britain and President Franklin D. Roosevelt had a good working relationship. In March 1941, Congress passed the Lend-Lease Act, which gave Roosevelt authority to send Churchill weapons, food, oil, and equipment. Congress hoped this costly service would take the form of defending the United States! America was still determined to stay out of the war!

Skill Level ★

Kansas City Star – 1940

*Another name was "Star X", from **Grandma Dexter**, a series
of booklets published in the early 1930s from the Virginia Snow
Studios, Elgin, Illinois.*

Supplies

12" Block
6" x 12" Ruler
6½" Triangle Square Up Ruler
6" Square Up Ruler
12½" Square Up Ruler

6" Block
6" x 12" Ruler
6½" Triangle Square Up Ruler
6" Square Up Ruler

	12" Finished Block	6" Finished Block
Background		
Corners	(1) 5" x 10"	(1) 3" x 6"
Star Points	(1) 5½" square	(1) 3½" square
Center	(1) 5½" square	(1) 3½" square
Medium		
Corners	(1) 5" x 10"	(1) 3" x 6"
Medium		
Center	(1) 5½" square	(1) 3½" square
Light Medium		
Star Points	(1) 5½" square	(1) 3½" square
Dark		
Star Points	(2) 5½" squares	(2) 3½" squares

Making One Center and Four Star Points

These patches are called quarter square patches.

1. Place three sets of squares right sides together. Draw diagonal lines.

12" Finished Block	6" Finished Block
5½" squares	3½" squares

Dark Star Points and Background

Dark Star Points and Light Medium Star Points

Medium Center and Background

2. Sew ¼" from both sides of diagonal line. Use 15 stitches per inch, or 2.0 on computerized machine.

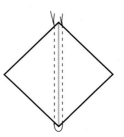 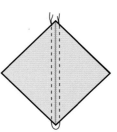 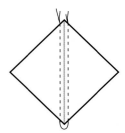

3. With rotary cutter and ruler, cut squares in half on diagonal line.

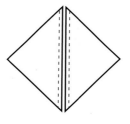 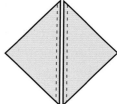 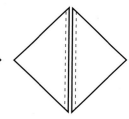

4. Set seams with darker on top.

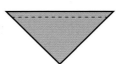 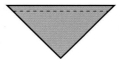 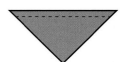

5. Open, and press seams toward medium and dark.

Make two sets of each.

6. Lay out sets. Flip patch on right to patch on left, right sides together.

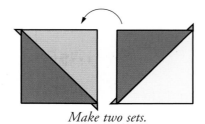

Make two sets.

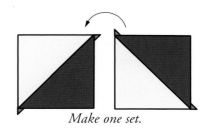

Make one set.

7. Lock center seams. Draw diagonal line.

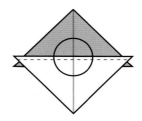

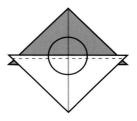

Lock center seams.

8. Assembly-line sew.

9. Cut on diagonal line.

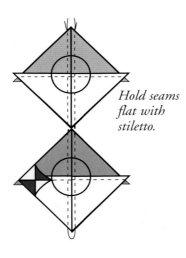

Hold seams flat with stiletto.

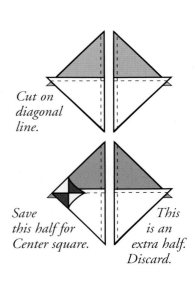

Cut on diagonal line.

Save this half for Center square.

This is an extra half. Discard.

10. Lock vertical seams.

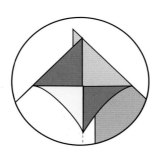

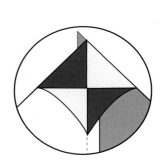

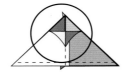

11. Square five patches with 6½" Triangle Square Up Ruler.

12" Finished Block	6" Finished Block
4½" squares	2½" squares

12" Block

Place **4½" red dashed line** on 6½" Triangle Square Up Ruler **above stitching line to compensate for fold**. Place ruler's diagonal line on vertical stitches. Trim two sides.

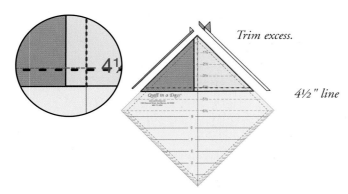

Trim excess.

4½" line

6" Block

Place **2½" red dashed line** on 6½" Triangle Square Up Ruler **above stitching line to compensate for fold**. Place ruler's diagonal line on vertical stitches. Trim two sides.

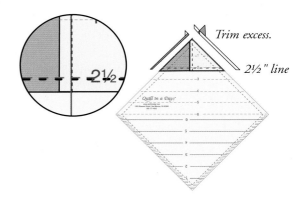

Trim excess.

2½" line

Four Star Points Only

1. Set seams with medium/dark Points on top. Open, and press seams.

2. Check that seam lines are centered in the corners.

3. Trim tips.

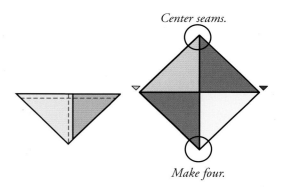

Center seams.

Make four.

Center Patch Only

*Pressing Center like this allows **all pieces** to lock when sewing block together.*

1. Use the one medium/Background patch that has been set aside.

2. Remove circled stitches on both sides shown in bright green.

3. Place on flat surface wrong side up.

4. Press top vertical seam to right, and bottom vertical seam to left. Open center, and press four-patch flat. Swirl seams around center.

5. Trim tips.

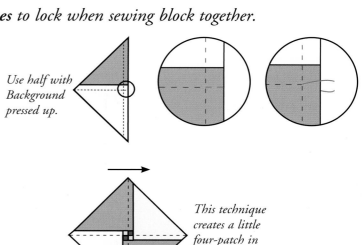

Use half with Background pressed up.

This technique creates a little four-patch in the center.

◩ Making Four Corners

1. Place Background rectangle right sides together to medium rectangle. Press.

12" Finished Block	6" Finished Block
5" x 10" rectangles	3" x 6" rectangles

2. Place on gridded cutting mat. Draw center line and one diagonal line in each square. Pin.

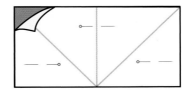

3. Sew ¼" from both sides of diagonal lines. Remove pins. Set seams.

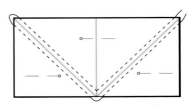

4. Cut apart on all drawn lines.

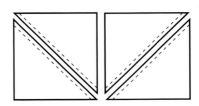

5. Square patches with 6½" Triangle Square Up Ruler.

12" Finished Block	6" Finished Block
4½" squares	2½" squares

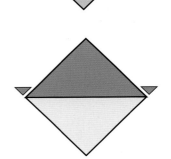

6. Set seam with medium on top, open, and press toward medium.

7. Trim tips.

🔲 Sewing Block Together

1. Lay out block.

2. Place Center patch so underneath seams are positioned as illustrated so all pieces lock together.

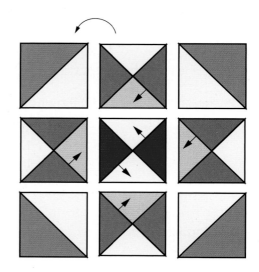

3. Flip middle vertical row to left vertical row. Assembly-line sew. Open. Do not clip connecting threads.

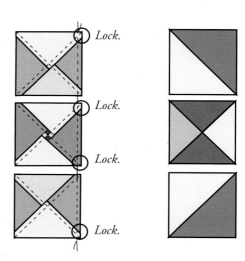

4. Flip right vertical row to middle vertical row. Assembly-line sew. Open.

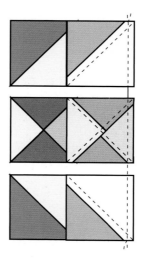

5. Turn. Flip right vertical row to middle vertical row. Push seams away from quarter square patches. Lock seams on top with seams underneath, and sew.

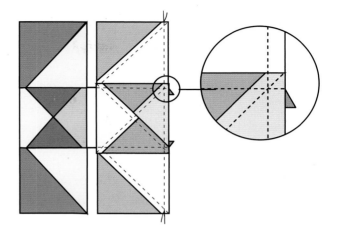

6. Sew remaining row, locking seams.

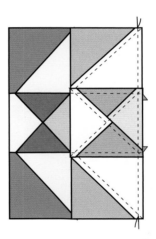

7. Press just sewn seams away from middle row.

8. Measure and record in box.

12" Finished Block

6" Finished Block

12½ " and 6½ " are ideal sizes
It is important that all blocks be
one consistent size.

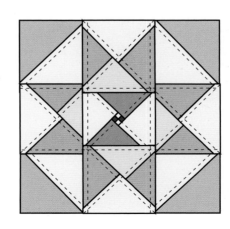

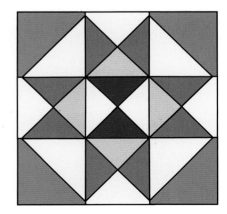

Fala

Fala, the best loved and most famous of all First Pets, belonged to President Franklin Roosevelt. The President loved Fala so much that he rarely went anywhere with out him.

The two were inseparable. Fala usually slept on a Navy blanket in the President's bedroom. When he played outdoors, it was within sight of Roosevelt's office window. Fala could be fed a treat if he rolled over, sat up and begged, plus a half dozen other tricks.

Fala progressed from a national to an international symbol of the United States, receiving thousands of love letters. Only death parted the Roosevelt and his dog. Fala outlived his master by seven years, and is buried at Hyde Park near him.

Portrait of President Roosevelt with Fala in the foreground

"These Republican leaders have not been content with attacks on me, or my wife, or on my sons. No, not content with that, they now include my little dog, Fala. Well, of course, I don't resent attacks, and my family doesn't resent them. You know, Fala is Scotch, and being Scottie, as soon as he learned that the Republican fiction writers in Congress and out had concocted a story that I had left him behind on the Aleutian Islands and had sent a destroyer back to find him—at a cost to taxpayers of two or three, or eight or twenty million dollars—his Scotch soul was furious. He has not been the same dog since. I am accustomed to hearing malicious falsehoods about myself—such as that old, worm-eaten chestnut that I have represented myself as indispensable. But I think I have a right to resent, to object to libelous statements about my dog."

Address to the Teamsters Union by President Roosevelt – September 23, 1944.

Skill Level ★

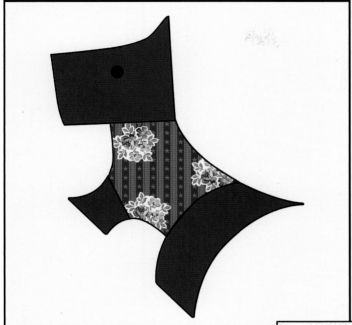

Layout for On Point Setting

Scottie Patchwork, #5673
Old Chelsea Station by Brooks and Wheeler
Gingham Dog, DuBois in Bye Baby Bunting
Fala, Telegraphics – 1976

Supplies

12" Block
Black Marking Pen
9" x 13" Light Weight
  Non-woven Fusible Interfacing
7" Square Template Plastic
Applique Tools - see page 16
Button

6" Block
Black Marking Pen
6" x 8" Light Weight
  Non-woven Fusible Interfacing
5" Square Template Plastic
Applique Tools - see page 16
Button

Layout for Straight Setting

	12" Finished Block	6" Finished Block
Background		
	(1) 12½" square	(1) 6½" square
Plaid		
Coat	(1) 6" square	(1) 3½" square
Dark		
Leg, Head, and Foot	(1) 9" square	(1) 6" square

Making Templates

1. Make photocopy of patterns. Rough cut around patterns.

2. Using glue stick, **put glue on printed side of paper.**

3. Place glued side of paper against template plastic, and rub in place.

4. Cut out on lines. If outside edges are rough, smooth with emery board.

   Seam allowance is already added to templates.

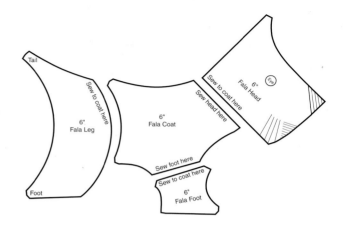

Cutting Out Pieces

1. **Turn plaid fabric wrong side up. Place Coat template on fabric right side up.** Trace around template, and cut on drawn lines.

12" Block	6" Block
6" square	3½" square

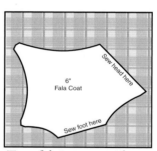

Turn fabric wrong side up. Place template on fabric wrong side up. Trace around template, and cut on draw line.

2. Trace Head, Leg, and Foot on wrong side of dark fabric with templates wrong side up, and cut on drawn lines.

3. Once pieces are cut, place templates back on them to make sure they are accurately cut.

12" Block	6" Block
9" square	6" square

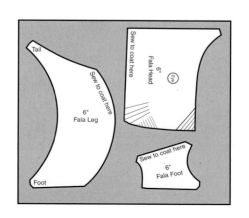

Sewing Pieces Together

1. Lay out pieces. Flip Coat right sides together to Head.

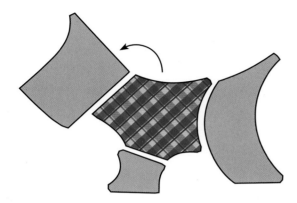

2. Sew with a ¼" seam.

3. Press seam toward Coat.

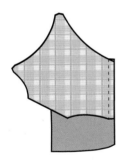

4. Place Foot with Coat/Head. Flip right sides together.

5. Sew and press seam toward Foot.

6. Place Leg with Coat/Head/Foot. Flip right sides together.

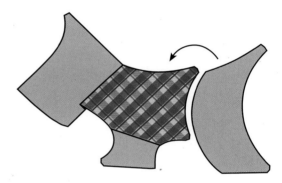

7. Line up and anchor seam with ½" of stitches.

8. Continue to sew, gently easing Leg to fit curve of Coat, and lining up outside edges.

9. Press seam toward Coat.

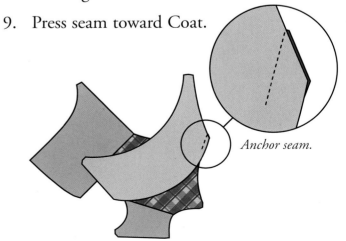

Anchor seam.

Finishing Outside Edges

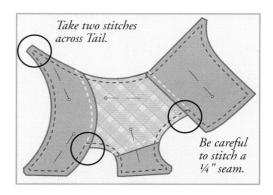

Take two stitches across Tail.

Be careful to stitch a ¼" seam.

1. Place fusible interfacing with bumpy fusible side up. Place Fala right sides together to fusible side. Pin.

12" Block	6" Block
9" x 13"	6" x 8"

2. Sew around outside edges with ¼" seam and 20 stitches per inch. Overlap beginning and ending stitches.

3. From interfacing side, trim ⅛" away from stitching. Trim corners, and clip inside curves.

4. Cut a small slit in the interfacing.

5. Insert straw into slit, and push against Ear fabric. Stretch fabric over end of straw. Place ball of bodkin on stretched fabric and **gently** push fabric into straw about 1" with bodkin. This technique begins to turn the piece.

6. Remove straw and bodkin. Repeat turning Nose, Tail, and Feet with straw and bodkin. Finish turning with fingers.

Push fabric into straw about 1" with bodkin.

7. Carefully push out edges by running bodkin or point turner around the inside.

8. Pick out points with stiletto or pin.

9. Press edges with wooden iron, or press on applique pressing sheet.

Choose placement to match your quilt setting.

Straight Set Block

1. Center on Background square.

2. Steam press in place.

12" Finished Block	6" Finished Block
12½" square	6½" square

It is important that all blocks be one consistent size.

Example of Blanket Stitch – Straight Set

On Point Block

1. Place on point with at least ¼" around outside edges.

2. Steam press in place.

Finishing Outside Edges

1. Finish outside edges by hand or machine. Use a hidden applique stitch by hand or a blind hem stitch with invisible thread by machine. It could also be finished with a blanket stitch using black floss or thread.

2. Hand embroider Whiskers and Nose. Sew on button Eye.

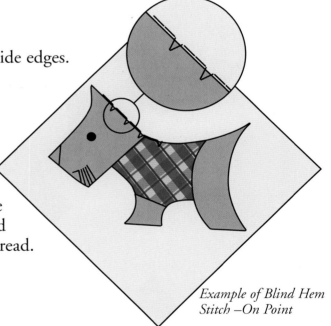

Example of Blind Hem Stitch – On Point

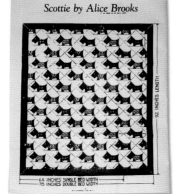

Scottie by Alice Brooks

Original Pattern

Mail order patterns were the answer for rural homemakers for most of the 20th century. Two popular collectible designers were Laura Wheeler and Alice Brooks. They designed needle craft patterns as well as simple aprons and linens, including the Scottie Dog pattern. The original Alice Brooks Scottie had eleven templates. By replacing seven Background templates with one square, the Scottie can be made with only four templates.

Puppy Dogs with Bone Border

The Bone Border is made of twenty 6" Mr. Roosevelt's Necktie blocks. The Dogs are 12" Fala blocks.

42" x 60"
Pieced by Patricia Knoechel
Quilted by Carol Selepec

Fabric Selection

Select one Background with small scale texture that reads solid. For the Bone Border, pair ¼ yd each of five different medium prints to five different dark prints for a total of ten ¼ yds or ten fat quarters. Vary the scales of the prints. Select one dark with small scale texture for Dogs. Use scraps from Bones for Dog Coats.

Twenty 6" Bone Blocks and Eight 12" Dog Blocks

Background	2¾ yds
Bone Blocks	(3) 2½" strips cut into (40) 2½" squares (8) 2" strips cut into (160) 2" squares
Dog Blocks	(3) 12½" strips cut into (8) 12½" squares
Setting Squares	(1) 6½" strip cut into (6) 6½" squares
Side Triangles	(1) 10" strip cut into (4) 10" squares
Corner Triangles	(1) 10" strip cut into (2) 10" squares

Bones and Coat	(5) ¼ yd pieces each of medium and dark
	Cut each into
Coat	(1) 6" square
Bones	(1) 2½" half strip cut into (6) 2½" squares
Bones	(1) 2" half strip cut into (8) 2" squares
Scrappy Binding	(1) 3" half strip plus (1) 3" half strip from any color

Dog	⅝ yd
Leg, Head, and Foot	(2) 9" strips cut into (8) 9" squares

One Color Binding	⅝ yd
(Optional)	(6) 3" strips

Backing	3¾ yds

Batting	50" x 68"

Non-Woven Fusible Interfacing	1½ yds cut (4) 13" strips into (8) 13" x 9"
Button Eyes	(8) ⅝" buttons
Collars	(8) 4½" pieces of trim or assorted beads

Supplies

Black Marking Pen
7" Square Template Plastic
Ball Point Bodkin
Fat Drinking Straw
Wooden Iron
5" Scissors

Making Twenty 6" Bone Blocks

1. Pair up one medium and one dark. Make five pairs. For each pair, count out this many:

2. From each pair, make four 6" Bone blocks following Mr. Roosevelt's Necktie, beginning on page 26.

Make Five Pairs		
Background	(8) 2½" squares	
	(32) 2" squares	
One Medium	(6) 2½" squares	
	(8) 2" squares	
One Dark	(6) 2½" squares	
	(8) 2" squares	

Making Eight 12" Dog Blocks

1. Make eight 12" Fala blocks following directions beginning on page 42. Sew on collars.

2. Steam press Dogs **on point** to 12½" Background squares.

3. Place Dogs in quilt layout.

Making Four Sets of Corner Blocks

1. Place Bones in quilt layout.

2. Sew two Bone blocks together for each corner.

3. Press seams to one side.

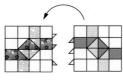

First two seams lock together. Third seams do not lock.

Example of upper left corner

4. For Corner Triangles, cut two 10" squares in half on one diagonal.

5. Center Corner on Corner Triangle, and assembly-line sew. Make four.

6. Press seams toward Corner Triangle. Trim tips.

7. **Place upper left and lower right Corners in quilt layout.**

8. For Side Triangles, cut four 10" squares on both diagonals.

9. Sew Side Triangle on each side of **upper right and lower left Corners.** Press seams toward Side Triangles. Trim tips.

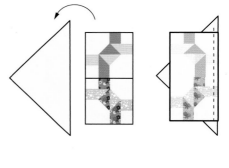

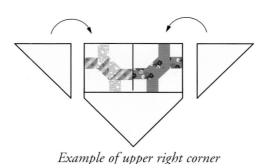

Example of upper right corner

Making Four Side Blocks

1. Sew one Side section at a time with two Bone blocks, one 6½" Background square, and two Side Triangles.

2. Sew vertical seams.

3. Press seams away from Bone blocks. Trim tips.

4. Sew horizontal rows. Press seam to one side.

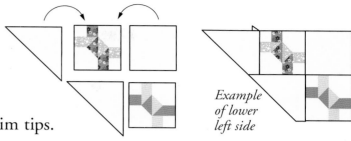

Example of lower left side

Making One Top and One Bottom Block

1. Lay out blocks.

2. Sew together following Side Blocks instruction.

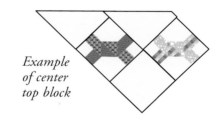

Example of center top block

Sewing Top Together

1. Lay out blocks in diagonal rows.

2. Sew blocks together, and press seams so blocks lock together.

3. Sew rows together. Press seams in one direction.

4. Square outside edges.

5. Piece 3" Scrappy Binding strips together.

6. Quilt and bind.

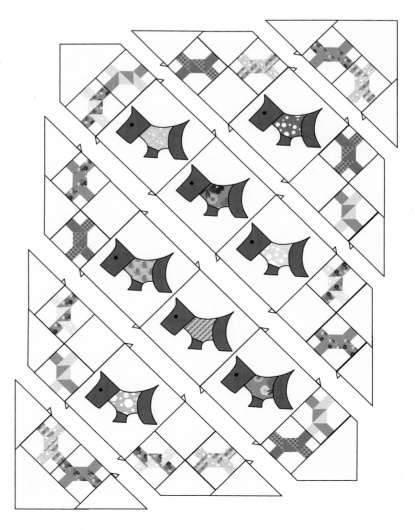

Comfort Quilt

Europe was devastated during World War II. Families often had to live in one room with no heat and blown out windows. Warmth was desperately needed! American and Canadian quilters were urged to make quilts for these destitute people. Church groups organized quilting bees, and were able to send thousands of quilts to Europe through the *United Nations, Red Cross, Lutheran, Mormon, and Mennonite* services, to name a few.

Heavy wool quilts were often made from old suits for war-torn Europe. These were usually tied, as they were too thick for quilting. Other quilts were simply strips from scraps or block patterns of log cabin, monkey wrench, bowtie and other familiar patterns. While most were utilitarian, some had cables hand quilted in the borders with diagonal lines across the center.

Attempts to get needed food and bedding to these people were thwarted by restrictions on what could be shipped to various regions that so much of the relief didn't get to the people until after the war was over.

Skill Level ★

Kansas City Star – 1940

Supplies

12" Block
12½" Square Up Ruler

6" Block
9½" Square Up Ruler

	12" Finished Block	6" Finished Block
Background		
Corners	(1) 3¼" x 14" cut into (4) 3¼" squares	(1) 1⅞" x 9" cut into (4) 1⅞" squares
Light		
Center Square	(1) 1½" square	(1) 1⅛" square
Nine-Patch	(1) 3¼" x 14" cut into (4) 3¼" squares	(1) 1⅞" x 9" cut into (4) 1⅞" squares
Medium		
Center Cross	(4) 1½" x 14" cut into (4) 1½" x 3¼"	(1) 1⅛" x 9" cut into (4) 1⅛" x 1⅞"
Dark		
Rectangles	(1) 3¼" x 29" cut into (4) 3¼" x 7"	(1) 1⅞" x 17" cut into (4) 1⅞" x 3¾"

⊞ Making Center Nine-Patch

1. Lay out one Center square, four squares for Nine-Patch, and four medium rectangles for Center Cross.

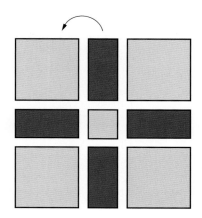

12" Finished Block	6" Finished Block
1½" square	1⅛" square
3¼" squares	1⅞" squares
1½" x 3¼" rectangles	1⅛" x 1⅞" rectangles

2. Flip middle vertical row to left vertical row, right sides together.

3. Assembly-line sew. Open. Do not clip connecting threads.

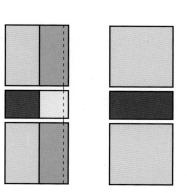

4. Flip right vertical row to middle vertical row, right sides together. Assembly-line sew.

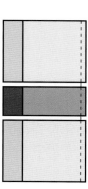

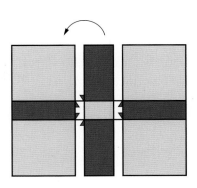

5. Turn. Sew remaining rows, pushing seams toward Center Cross and locking seams.

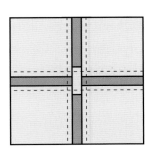

6. Press just sewn seams toward Center.

7. Measure patchwork. Sliver trim or resew if necessary.

12" Finished Block	6" Finished Block
7" square	3¾" square

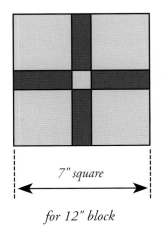

7" square

for 12" block

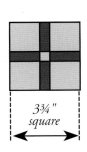

3¾" square

for 6" block

▦ Sewing Block Together

1. Lay out Center Nine-Patch, four Background Corner squares, and dark Rectangles.

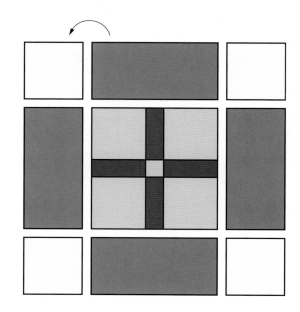

12" Finished Block	6" Finished Block
3¼" squares	1⅞" squares
3¼" x 7" rectangles	1⅞" x 3¾" rectangles

2. Flip middle vertical row to left vertical row, right sides together.

3. Assembly-line sew. Open. Do not clip connecting threads.

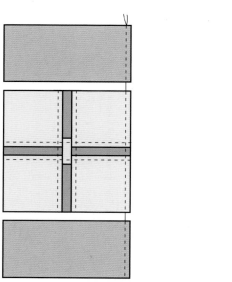

4. Flip right vertical row to middle vertical row right sides together, and assembly-line sew.

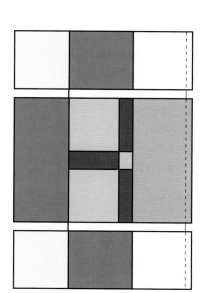

5. Turn. Sew remaining rows, pushing seams toward Rectangles and locking seams.

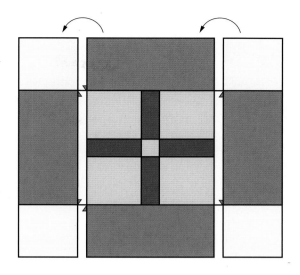

6. Press just sewn seams away from center.

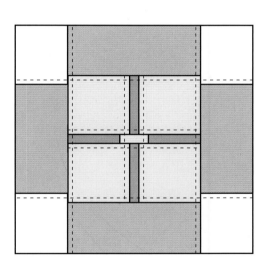

7. Measure and record in box.

12" Finished Block	6" Finished Block

12½" is ideal size   *6½" is ideal sizes*
It is important that all blocks be one consistent size.

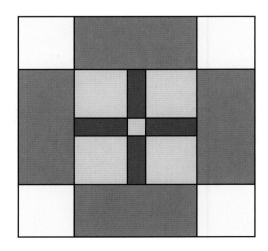

Scrappy Friendship Quilt

Group Quilting Party

Each month at Quilt in a Day, women gather for Block Party. Through the years, we've shared lasting friendships as well as learn new quilting techniques. In 2007, each of us made a Comfort block in patriotic fabrics to support our brave men and women defending our country.

If you have a friend you wish to honor, sponsor a Comfort Quilt Party. Photocopy cutting instructions on page 53 and dispense to friends ahead of time. Ask guests to cut pieces in specified color scheme from their scraps. If necessary, ask them to make more than one block. Stand up and salute your friend with pride!

78" x 94"
32 Blocks
Top assembled
by Teresa Varnes
Quilted by
Judy Jackson

	Eighteen 12" Finished Blocks 60" x 76"	Thirty-two 12" Finished Blocks 78" x 94"
Yellow	**1 yd**	**1¾ yds**
Lattice	(16) 2" strips cut into (48) 2" x 12½" or size of block	(27) 2" strips cut into (80) 2" x 12½" or size of block
Red	**¼ yd**	**¼ yd**
Cornerstones	(2) 2" strips cut into (31) 2" squares	(3) 2" strips cut into (49) 2" squares
Blue	**2 yds**	**2½ yds**
Side Triangles	(3) 21" squares Cut on both diagonals	(4) 21" squares Cut on both diagonals
Corner Triangles	(2) 11½" squares Cut one diagonal	(2) 11½" squares Cut one diagonal
Red	**⅔ yd**	**1 yd**
Binding	(7) 3" strips	(9) 3" strips
Backing	4 yds	5¾ yds
Batting	68" x 82"	86" x 102"

Eighteen 12" Finished Blocks 60" x 76"

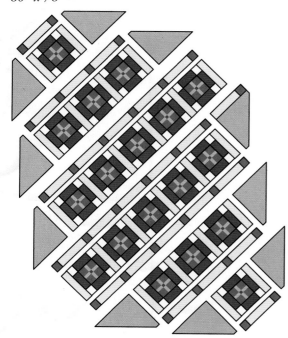

Thirty-two 12" Finished Blocks 78" x 94"

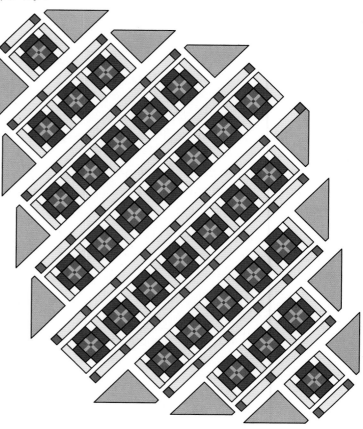

Follow directions starting on pages 208 for sewing Eighteen Block On Point Quilt together.

1941 Nine-Patch

Illustration courtesy of Simmons Bedding Company

Life was good in 1941. High priority was placed on marriage and family. Women were the backbone of the family, staying home to take care of household duties and raise the children. The American population felt that if a woman was married and her husband had a job, she did not need to work outside the home.

Men were the head of the house, the protector, and the breadwinner. He made a minimum wage of $.43 an hour, or an average yearly salary of $1,299. Monogamy reigned! Divorce was difficult if not impossible to obtain.

In 1941, only 15% of college age population attended college. One third of all households were still cooking with wood or coal. Only 55% of homes in the United States had indoor plumbing.

One home in seven had a telephone, 40% had central heating, and 75% had a refrigerator or ice box. Only one out of five Americans owned a car. Life was good in 1941!

My parents, Erwin and Erma, eloped in 1941. Mother told the story about how her grandmother gave her $100 for a bed, but Father spent it on a down-payment for a car named Blue Bird, short for Blue Bird of Happiness. He was one of the lucky ones out of five Americans to own a car.

Skill Level ★ ★

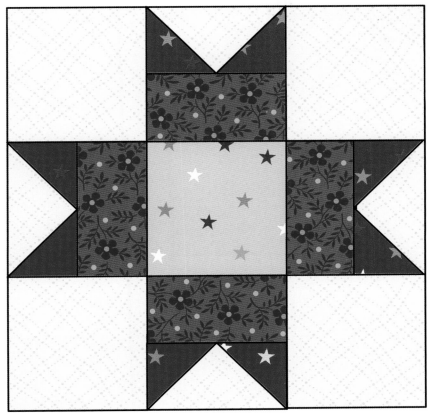

Kansas City Star – 1941

Supplies

12" Block
Mini Flying Geese Ruler One
   for 2" x 4" Finished Size Geese
4" x 14" Ruler
Small Cutting Mat

6" Block
Mini Flying Geese Ruler One
   for 1" x 2" Finished Size Geese
4" x 14" Ruler
Small Cutting Mat

	12" Finished Block	6" Finished Block
Background		
Star Points	(1) 5½" square	(1) 3½" square
Corners	(1) 4½" x 19" cut into	(1) 2½" x 11" cut into
	(4) 4½" squares	(4) 2½" squares
Light Medium		
Center	(1) 4½" square	(1) 2½" square
Medium		
Rectangles	(1) 2½" x 19" cut into	(1) 1½" x 11" cut into
	(4) 2½" x 4½"	(4) 1½" x 2½"
Dark		
Star Points	(1) 7" square	(1) 5" square

◥◣ Making Star Points

*Star Points are made with a patch called Geese Patch.
One set of squares makes four Star Points.*

1. Place smaller Background square right sides together and centered on larger Star Points square. Press.

12" Finished Block	6" Finished Block
5½" square	3½" square
7" square	5" square

2. Place ruler on squares so ruler touches all four corners. Draw diagonal line across squares.

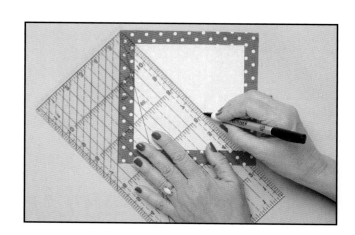

3. Pin squares together. Sew ¼" on both sides of drawn line. Use 15 stitches per inch or 2.0 on computerized machines.

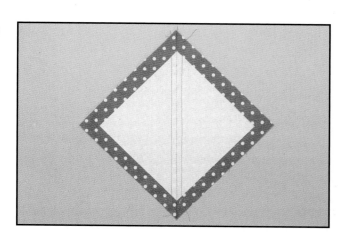

4. Remove pins. Cut on drawn line.

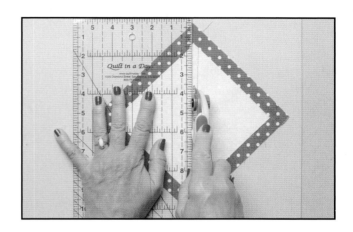

5. Place on pressing mat with large triangle on top. Press to set seam.

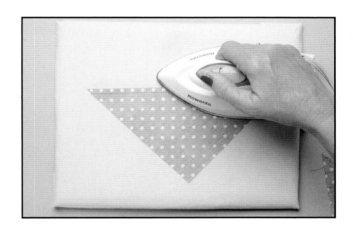

6. Open and press flat. Check that there are no tucks, and seam is pressed toward larger triangle.

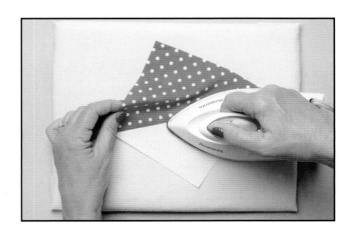

7. Place pieces right sides together so that opposite fabrics touch with Background matched to Star Points. Seams are parallel with each other.

8. Match outside edges. There is a gap between seams.

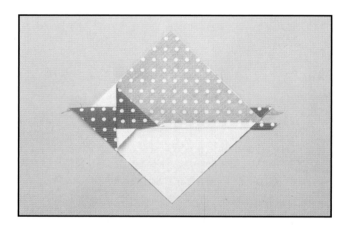

9. Draw a diagonal line across seams. Pin.

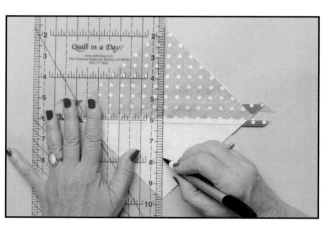

10. Sew ¼" from both sides of drawn line. Hold seams flat with stiletto so seams do not flip. Press to set seam.

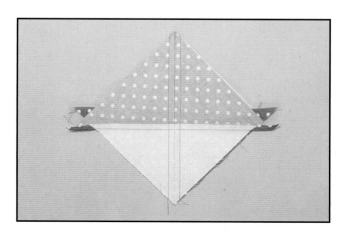

11. Cut on drawn line.

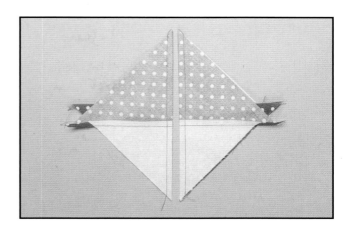

12. Fold in half. Clip seam allowance to vertical seam midway between horizontal seams. This allows the seam allowance to be pressed toward Star Points.

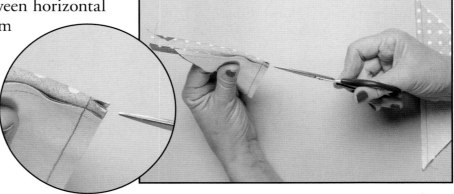

13. From right side, press into one Star Point. Turn and press into second Star Point.

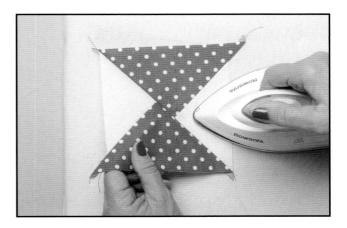

14. Turn over, and press on wrong side. At clipped seam, fabric is pressed toward Star Points.

Squaring Up 12" Block with Mini Geese Ruler One

1. Place InvisiGRIP™ on bottom side of 2" x 4" Mini Geese Ruler One.

2. Place patch on small cutting mat so you can rotate mat as you cut. Place 2" x 4" ruler on patch. **Line up ruler's green solid lines for 2" x 4" Finished Geese on sewn lines.** Line up green dashed line with peak of triangle for ¼" seam.

3. Hold ruler securely on fabric so it doesn't shift while cutting.

4. Cut block in half to separate two patches.

5. Trim off excess fabric on right.

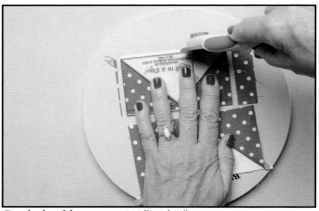

6. Turn mat. Trim off excess fabric on right and top. **Patch should measure 2½" x 4½".**

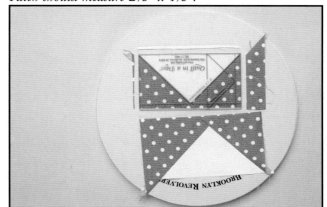

Patch should measure 2½" x 4½".

7. Repeat with remaining half.

Squaring Up 6" Block with Mini Geese Ruler One

1. Place InivisiGRIP™ on bottom side of 2" x 4" Mini Geese Ruler One.

2. Place patch on small cutting mat. **Line up ruler's red solid lines for 1" x 2" Finished Geese on sewn lines.** Line up red dashed line with peak of triangle for ¼" seam allowance.

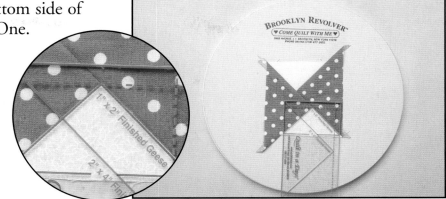

3. Cut block in half to separate two patches.

4. Trim off excess fabric on right. Hold ruler securely on fabric so it doesn't shift while cutting.

5. Turn patch around. Do not turn ruler. Trim off excess fabric on right and top. **Patch should measure 1½" x 2½".**

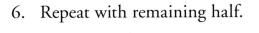
Patch should measure 1½" x 2½".

6. Repeat with remaining half.

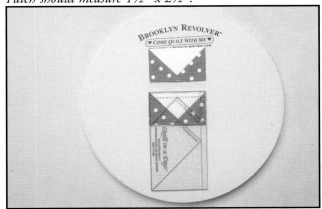

Squaring Up without Mini Geese Ruler One for 12" and 6" Blocks

1. With 6" x 12" Ruler, line up 45° line on diagonal seam, and ¼" line on peak.

2. Cut across, keeping an exact ¼" seam allowance beyond peak.

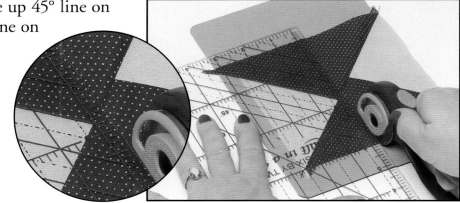

3. With 6" Square Up Ruler, place diagonal line on seam. Line up bottom edge of patch with horizontal line on ruler. Line up vertical line with peak. Trim right and top edges.

12" Finished Block	6" Finished Block
2½" horizontal line	1½" horizontal line
2¼" vertical line	1¼" vertical line

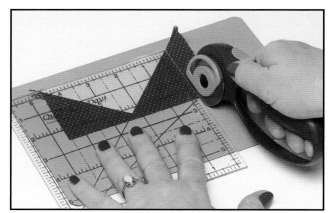

Example of 12" block at 2½" horizontal line and 2¼" vertical line

4. Turn patch. Trim remaining side.

12" Finished Block	6" Finished Block
2½" x 4½"	1½" x 2½"

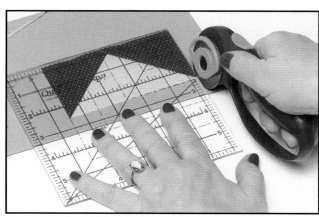

Example of 12" block at 2½" x 4½"

◤ Sewing Star Points with Rectangles

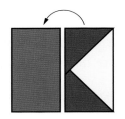

1. Stack four Star Points next to four Rectangles.

2. Flip right sides together with Star Points on top.

12" Finished Block	6" Finished Block
2½" x 4½" Star Points	1½" x 2½" Star Points
2½" x 4½" Rectangles	1½" x 2½" Rectangles

3. Assembly-line sew with a ¼" seam.

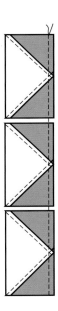

4. Press seam away from Star Points.

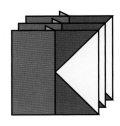 

Sewing Block Together

1. Lay out four Background squares, four Star Points and one Center Square.

12" Finished Block	6" Finished Block
4½" squares	2½" squares

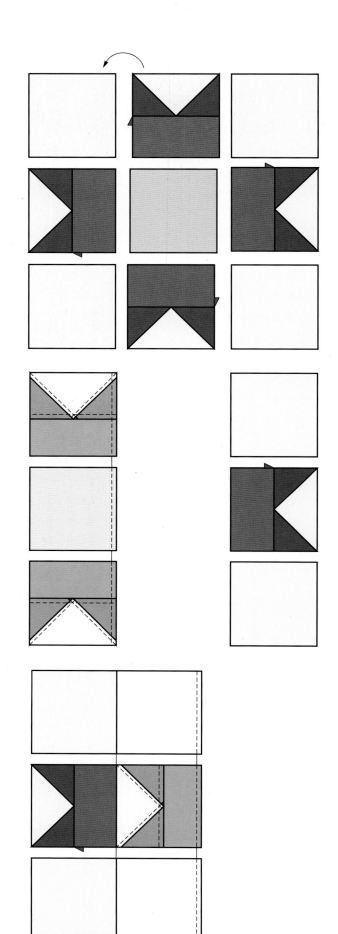

2. Flip middle vertical row to left vertical row, right sides together.

3. Assembly-line sew. Open. Do not clip connecting threads.

4. Flip right vertical row to middle vertical row right sides together, and assembly-line sew. Do not clip connecting threads.

5. Turn. Sew remaining rows, pushing seams away from Star Points, locking seams.

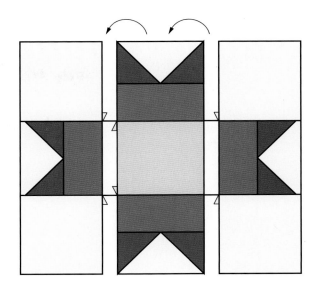

6. Press just sewn seams away from center.

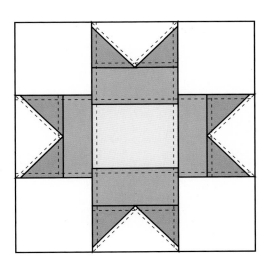

7. Measure and record in box.

12" Finished Block	6" Finished Block

12½" is ideal size   *6½" is ideal size*
It is important that all blocks be one consistent size.

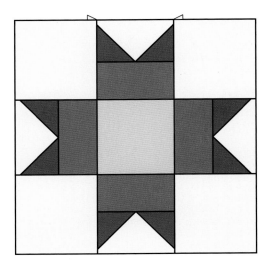

...dio Windmill

...decades, women listened to the radio while cleaning and ...ning. Most of them listened to the daily dramatic serials ... "soap operas" because many of them were sponsored by ... of soap and other household cleaners. Rinso had "Big ... One of the longest-lasting soaps was "Oxydol's own ...kins."

..., 90% of sponsored network programming during the day was soap operas. In 1948, of the top ...grams on radio, 25 were soaps, including the top ten.

...were divided into ten plots as #1: "The woman who struggles to maintain orderliness and provide ... brood against imposing odds such as a worthless or absent spouse, crushing economic blows, ... out-of-control adolescent offspring." Not all daytime serials were misery-based, such as "Vic and ..."Lorenzo Jones," and "Ethel and Albert." Then there was the Romance of Helen Trent, with her ...s recordings in 1940's. One of her programs was titled, "Helen faints beside a corpse."

Skill Level ★

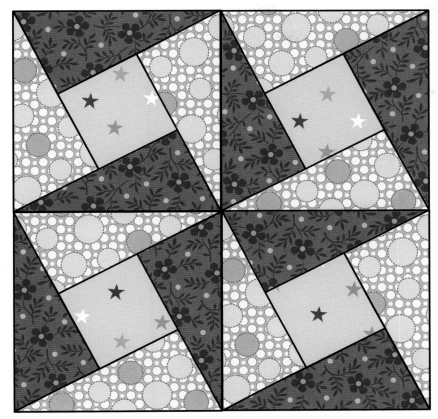

Kansas City Star – 1941
Windmill, Nancy Cabot

Supplies

12" Block
6½" Fussy Cut Ruler
6" x 12" Ruler
Rotating Mat

6" Block
3½" Fussy Cut Ruler
6" x 12" Ruler
Rotating Mat

	12" Finished Size	6" Finished Size
Light		
Center Squares	(1) 3¼" x 14" cut into (4) 3¼" squares	(1) 2" x 9" cut into (4) 2" squares
Medium		
Set of Blades	(1) 3½" x 28" cut into (4) 3½" x 6¾"	(1) 2¼" x 19" cut into (4) 2¼" x 4½"
Dark		
Set of Blades	(1) 3½" x 28" cut into (4) 3½" x 6¾"	(1) 2¼" x 19" cut into (4) 2¼" x 4½"

Sewing Four Patches

The technique used to sew the block is called partial seaming.

1. Stack four medium and four dark Rectangles **right side up**, and cut on diagonal.

12" Finished Block	6" Finished Block
3½" x 6¾" rectangles	2¼" x 4½" rectangles

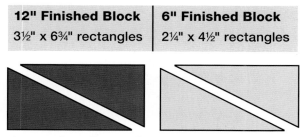

Cut exactly as illustrated. If cut in the opposite direction, all pieces will be mirror image.

2. Lay out block with Center Squares. Numbers represent position of pieces.

12" Finished Block	6" Finished Block
3¼" squares	2" squares

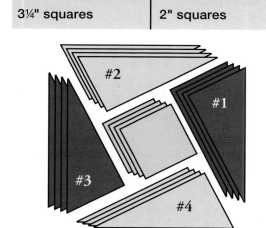

3. Flip #1 right sides together to Center Square.

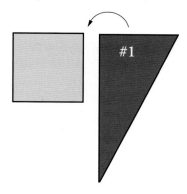

4. With ¼" seam sew, ¾ of way and stop sewing. Repeat with remaining three.

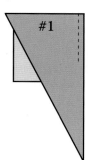

5. Press #1 seam away from Center Square.

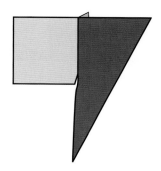

6. Turn patch. Place #2 beside patch. Flip #2 right sides together to Center Square.

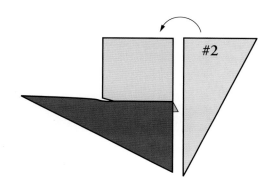

7. Line up straight edges. Assembly-line sew.

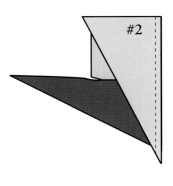

8. Press #2 seam away from Center Square.

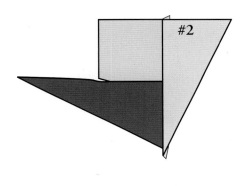

9. Turn patch. Place #3 beside patch. Flip #3 right sides together to Center Square.

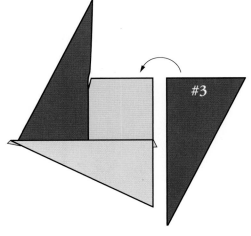

10. Line up straight edges. Assembly-line sew.

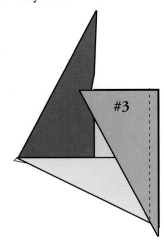

11. Press #3 seam away from Center Square.

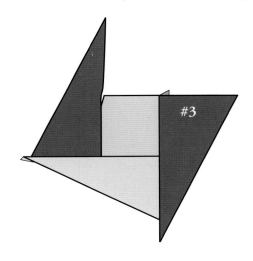

12. Turn patch. Place #4 beside patch.

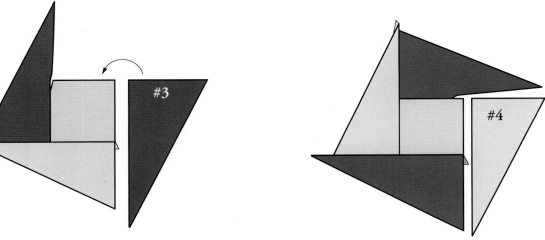

13. Fold #1 out of the way. Flip #4 right sides together to Center Square. Line up straight edges, and sew length of seam. Press #4 seam away from Center Square.

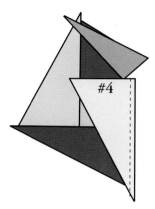

14. Turn patch. Flip #1 right sides together to #4. Continue sewing #1. Press #1 seam away from Center Square.

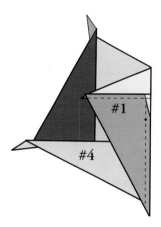

15. Check on back side. All seams are pressed away from Center Square.

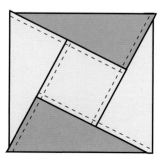

◪ Squaring Four Patches

1. Place Fussy Cut Ruler on patch.

12" Finished Block	6" Finished Block
6½" Fussy Cut Ruler	3½" Fussy Cut Ruler

2. Carefully line up four corner squares on ruler with diagonal seams. Manipulate fabric under ruler if necessary.

3. Place on a rotating mat. Trim on four sides, turning mat as you trim.

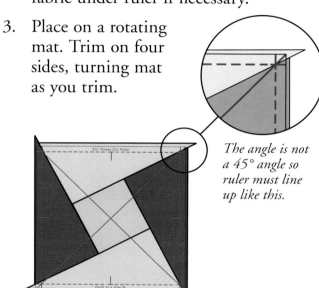

The angle is not a 45° angle so ruler must line up like this.

4. From right side, check that seams are ⅛" from corners.

⅛"

Seams do not go into corners.

Sewing Four Patches Together

1. Lay out four blocks with "pinwheel" in center.

2. Flip vertical row on right to vertical row on left.

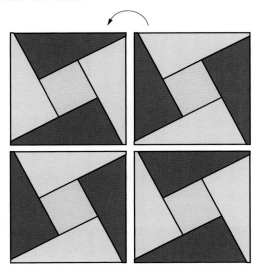

3. Pin ¼" in from edges, matching seams.

4. Assembly-line sew. Do not clip connecting threads.

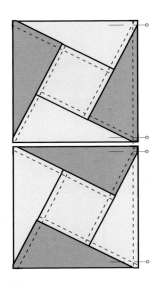

5. Turn, and sew remaining row. At connecting thread, push top seam up, and underneath seam down.

6. Clip connecting thread, and remove approximately three straight stitches on both sides. See green thread.

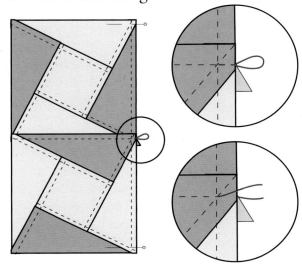

7. Lay block flat wrong side up.

8. Swirl seams to the right around center. Remove stitches in center and press center open. Flatten. Center looks like a pinwheel.

9. Measure and record in box.

12" Finished Block	6" Finished Block
12½" is ideal size	*6½" is ideal size*

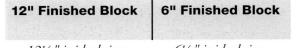

It is important that all blocks be one consistent size.

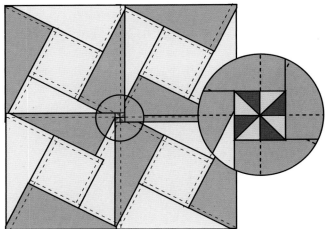

Sky Rocket

Lined up in Battleship Row was the United States fleet in Pearl Harbor, the main target of the attack by the Japanese on December 7, 1941. The attack came in two waves, the first at 7:53 AM and the second at 8:55 AM. The strike that Sunday morning left 2,403 dead, 188 destroyed airplanes, and a crippled Pacific Fleet. In response to the attack, the United States declared war on Japan, bringing America into World War II.

The attack on Pearl Harbor stirred the hearts of Americans more forcefully than any other single event. It was regarded as an atrocious surprise attack and an act of dishonor. During the War, every effort was made to keep the memory of the attack on Pearl Harbor alive and in the minds of Americans. Posters, popular songs and other media were staples of wartime popular culture, regular memorial services were held to commemorate the dead, and flags that had flown at the Capitol and White House on December 7, 1941 were raised over fallen enemy capital cities.

Now, Pearl Harbor War Memorial and Visitor's Center is a National Park. Over 1.5 million people visit the Memorial and its museum and over 30,000 school children participate in its education program each year.

Skill Level ★ ★ ★

Sky Rocket, Ruby McKim
Starlight, Nancy Page
Jewel Boxes, Nancy Page
The Album, Kansas City Star – 1937

Supplies

12" Block
6" x 12" Ruler
12½" Square Up Ruler
6" Square Up Ruler
Template plastic
Pins
Marking Pen

6" Block
6" x 12" Ruler
6½" Triangle Square Up Ruler
6" Square Up Ruler
Template plastic
Pins
Marking Pen

	12" Finished Block	6" Finished Block
Background		
Rocket Points	(2) 2¾" x 40" strips cut into (8) 2¾" x 8¼"	(1) 1¾" x 40" strip cut into (8) 1¾" x 5"
Light		
Star Points	(1) 2" x 17" strip cut into (8) 2" squares	(1) 1¼" x 11" strip cut into (8) 1¼" squares
Star Center	(1) 3⅜" square	(1) 1⅞" square
Medium		
Rockets	(1) 3⅜" x 15" strip cut into (4) 3⅜" squares	(1) 1⅞" x 9" strip cut into (4) 1⅞" squares
Rocket Points	(2) 5¼" x 6"	(2) 3¼" x 3¾"
Dark		
Corner Squares	(1) 3⅜" x 15" strip cut into (4) 3⅜" squares	(1) 1⅞" x 9" strip cut into (4) 1⅞" squares

Making Star Points

1. Turn eight Star Point squares wrong side up.
   If available, place on top of sandpaper.

12" Finished Block	6" Finished Block
2" squares	1¼" squares

2. With pencil, draw diagonal line corner to corner.

3. Place open toe applique foot on sewing machine. Set
   needle in center position, and use 2.0 stitch length.

4. Place Star Point square right sides
   together to Rocket square.

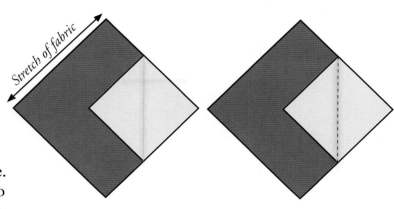

12" Finished Block	6" Finished Block
3⅜" square	1⅞" square

5. Sew on **right side of diagonal line**.
   Assembly-line sew four squares. To
   avoid jamming, begin sewing on a
   scrap.

6. Set seam. Trim ¼" away from stitched diagonal line.

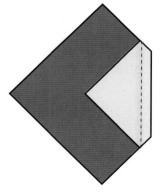

7. Open triangle and press toward Star Point.

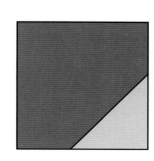

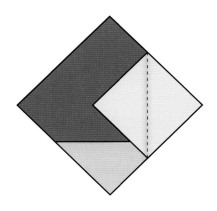

8. Place Star Point square on adjacent corner of Rocket square, right sides together.

12" Finished Block	6" Finished Block
2" square	1¼" square

9. Assembly-line sew to right of diagonal line.

10. Set seam. Trim ¼" away from stitched diagonal line.

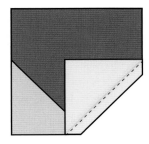

11. Open triangle and press toward Star Point.

12. Check stitching on back side.

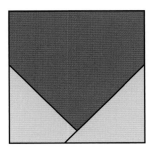
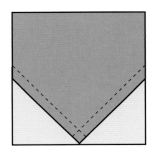

13. If necessary, square with 6" Square Up Ruler without trimming away ¼" seam allowance.

12" Finished Block	6" Finished Block
3⅜" square	1⅞" square

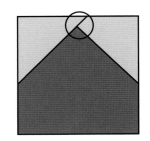

✳ Finishing Center Patch

1. Change back to quarter inch foot on sewing machine.

2. Lay out Star Points with one Center square and four Corner squares.

12" Finished Block	6" Finished Block
3⅜" squares	1⅞" squares

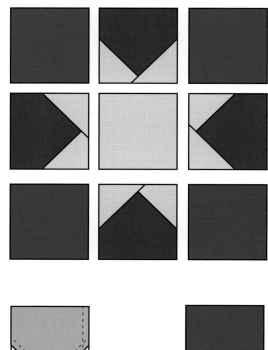

3. Flip middle vertical row to left vertical row.

4. Assembly-line sew. Do not clip connecting threads. Open.

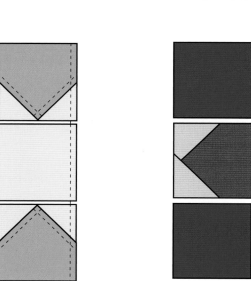

5. Flip right vertical row to middle vertical row and assembly-line sew. Do not clip connecting threads.

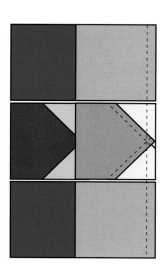

6. Sew remaining rows, locking seams and pressing seams away from Star Points.

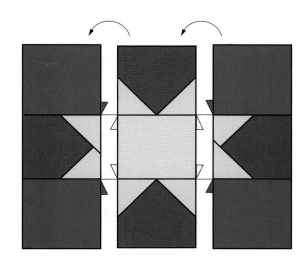

7. Press just sewn seams away from center.

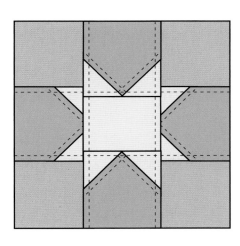

8. Measure Center Patch. These are approximate measurements.

12" Finished Block	6" Finished Block
9⅛" square	4¾" square

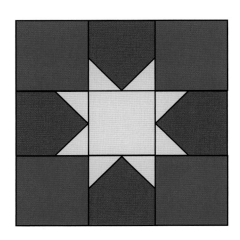

▼ Cutting Rockets

1. Photocopy template, glue to template plastic, and cut out with ruler and rotary cutter.

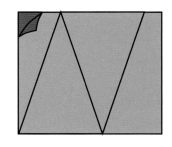

2. Place two rocket pieces right sides together.

12" Finished Block	6" Finished Block
5¼" x 6"	3¼" x 3¾"

3. Trace two sets of Rockets with template.

4. Cut on lines with rotary cutter. Discard extra.

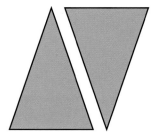

◹ Cutting Background for Rockets

1. Stack one pair of Background **wrong sides together**.

12" Finished Block	6" Finished Block
2¾" x 8¼"	1¾" x 5"

2. Place 45° diagonal line on 6" Square Up Ruler across top of left end, and layer cut. Discard corners.

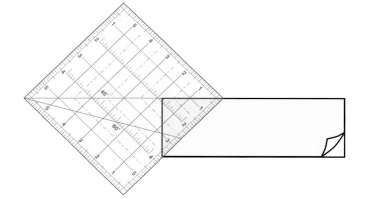

3. Layer cut from peak to corner with 6" x 12" Ruler. Discard corners.

4. Repeat with remaining pairs.

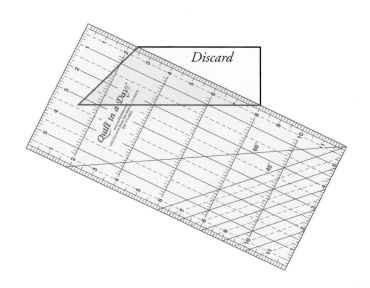

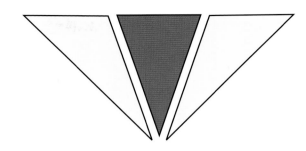 **Sewing Rockets Together**

1. Stack all pieces right side up. Background pieces are mirror image.

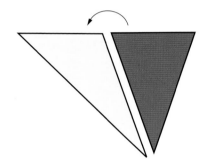

2. Set right stack of Background triangles aside.

3. Flip Rocket triangle right sides together to left Background triangle. Let ⅛" tip from Rocket triangle hang over on top. Assembly-line sew.

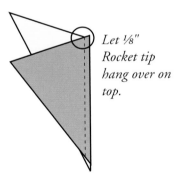

Let ⅛" Rocket tip hang over on top.

4. Set seam with Background on top. Open, and press toward Background.

5. Line up ruler with side of Rocket triangle. Trim Background tip with ruler and rotary cutter.

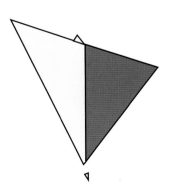

6. Place right stack of Background triangles beside Rocket triangles.

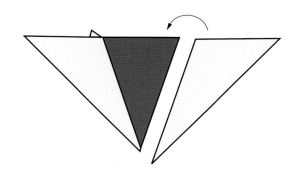

7. Flip Background triangle right sides together to Rocket triangle. Let ⅛" tip from Rocket hang over on top. Assembly-line sew.

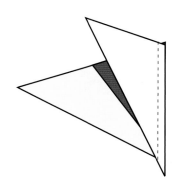

8. Set seam with Background on top. Open, and press toward Background.

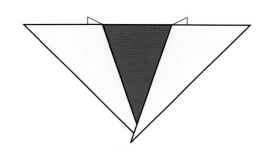

9. Check seams on back side.

10. If necessary, straighten top by sliver trimming. **Do not trim tips.**

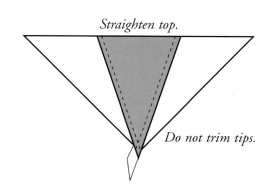

Straighten top.

Do not trim tips.

✦ Sewing Block Together

1. Place Rockets wrong side up around Center Patch.

2. Mark ¼" in from straight edge on **wrong side of Rockets**.

3. Mark ¼" in on **right side** of Center Patch.

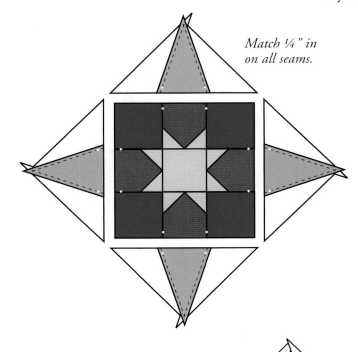

Match ¼" in on all seams.

4. **Flip Rocket right sides together to patch.** Center Rocket on Rocket square, and line up seams. Insert pins ¼" in from edge and sew.

5. Check to see that seams match.

6. Set seam with Rocket on top, open, and press seam toward Rocket. Trim tips even with Center Patch.

7. Sew Rocket to opposite side of Center Patch. Trim tips.

8. Add remaining two Rockets in same manner.

9. Square block without trimming away ¼" seam allowance on corners.

12" Finished Block	6" Finished Block
12½" Square Up Ruler	6½" Triangle Square Up Ruler

10. Measure and record in box.

12" Finished Block	6" Finished Block

12½" is ideal size   *6½" is ideal size*
It is important that all blocks be one consistent size.

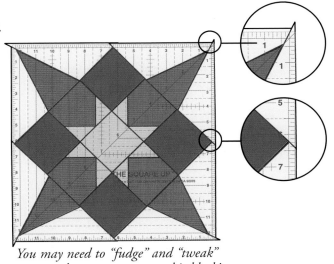

You may need to "fudge" and "tweak" corners when you square up this block!

Sky Rocket Tablerunner

28" x 58"
Pieced by Eleanor Burns
Quilted by Amie Potter

Three 12" Finished Blocks

Background	1¼ yds
Three Blocks	(6) 2¾" strips cut into (24) 2¾" x 8¼" rectangles
Lattice	(6) 3⅜" strips cut into (10) 3⅜" x 12½" (12) 3⅜" x 6"

Light	½ yd
Star Points	(5) 2" strips cut into (88) 2" squares
Star Center	(1) 3⅜" strip cut into (11) 3⅜" squares

Medium	¾ yd
Rockets	(1) 3⅜" strip cut into (12) 3⅜" squares
Rocket Points	(1) 5¼" strip cut into (6) 5¼" x 6"
Binding	(5) 3" strips

Dark	1 yd
Squares Borders	(1) 3⅜" strip cut into (12) 3⅜" squares
	(4) 6" strips cut into (8) 6" x 12½" (4) 6" squares

Backing	1¾ yds
Batting	32" x 62"

Making Tablerunner

1. Turn eighty-eight 2" Star Point squares wrong side up, and draw a diagonal line corner to corner on each square. *To save time marking diagonal lines, sew using an Angler.*

2. Sew three Sky Rocket blocks following directions beginning on page 80.

3. Sew Star Points on one end of twelve 3⅜" x 6" Background Lattice.

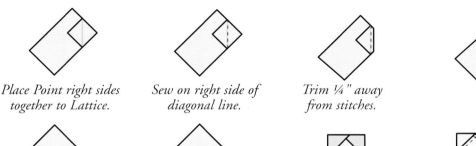

Place Point right sides together to Lattice.   *Sew on right side of diagonal line.*   *Trim ¼ " away from stitches.*   *Open and press toward Point.*

Place Point on adjacent corner.   *Sew on right side of line and trim.*   *Open and press toward Point.*   *Check on back side.*

4. Sew Star Points on both ends of ten 3⅜" x 12½" Background Lattice.

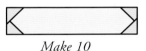

Make 10

5. Lay out three blocks with eight 3⅜" Star Centers, Lattice with Star Points, and 6" Border.

6. Sew Tablerunner together in vertical rows.

7. Sew remaining rows, pressing seams away from Lattice.

8. Quilt and bind.

Contrary Wife

Prior to the war, women generally held jobs that were either low paying, or held little appeal for male workers. Once the men went off to war, the shortage of labor occurred in much higher paying jobs. Women saw the situation as a wonderful opportunity for them to excel financially, and gain more independence and freedom. For the first time in United States history, married women outnumbered single women workers.

Eighty percent of women in war industry jobs were hoping to keep these jobs after the war ended. However, once soldiers began returning home, they wanted their jobs back. The prewar employment pattern was re-established and most employed women returned to stereotypical women's jobs of clerical or domestic services.

Skill Level ★

Kansas City Star – 1941

Supplies

12" Block
6" x 12" Ruler
6½" Triangle Square Up Ruler
12½" Square Up Ruler

6" Block
6" Square Up Ruler
6" x 12" Ruler
6½" Triangle Square Up Ruler

	12" Finished Block	6" Finished Block
Background		
Triangles	(1) 5" x 10"	(1) 3" x 6"
Light		
Triangles	(1) 5" x 10"	(1) 3" x 6"
Medium		
Two Squares	(2) 4½" squares	(2) 2½" squares
Dark		
Three Squares	(1) 4½" x 14" strip cut into	(1) 2½" x 8" strip cut into
	(3) 4½" squares	(3) 2½" squares

Making Four Triangle Pieced Squares

1. Place Background right sides together to light Triangle.

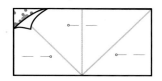

12" Finished Block	6" Finished Block
5" x 10"	3" x 6"

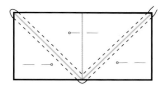

2. Draw a center line.

3. Draw diagonal lines. Pin.

4. Sew a ¼" seam on both sides of diagonal lines. Press.

5. Cut apart on drawn lines.

6. Square with 6½" Square Up Ruler.

12" Finished Block	6" Finished Block
4½" squares	2½" squares

12" Block

Place 4½" **red dashed line** on 6½" Triangle Square Up Ruler slightly **above stitching line** to compensate for fold. Center ruler on patch. Trim two sides.

6" Block

Place 2½" **red dashed line** on 6½" Triangle Square Up Ruler **above stitching line** to compensate for fold. Center ruler on patch. Trim two sides.

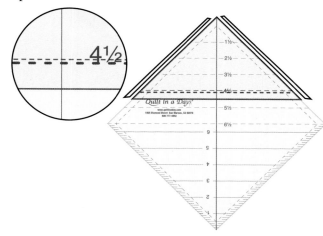

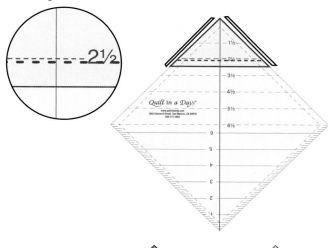

7. Set seam with medium on top.

8. Open, and press seams toward medium.

9. Trim tips.

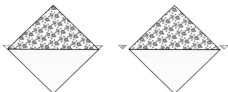

⊞ Sewing Block Together

1. Lay out pieces.

2. Flip middle vertical row right sides together to left vertical row.

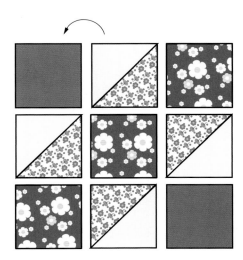

3. Assembly-line sew. Do not clip connecting threads. Open.

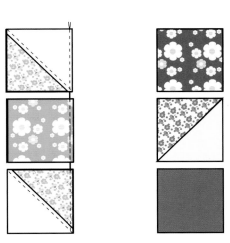

4. Flip right vertical row to middle vertical row, and assembly-line sew. Do not clip connecting threads. Open.

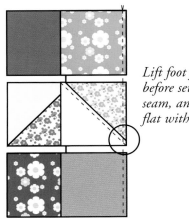

Lift foot just before sewing over seam, and hold flat with stiletto.

5. Turn block. Flip right vertical row to middle row.

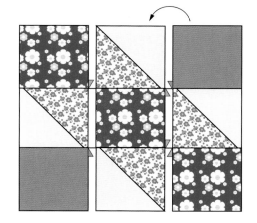

6. Press seams away from triangle pieced squares, lock seams and assembly-line sew.

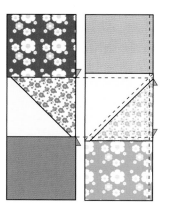

7. Repeat on remaining row.

8. Press just sewn seams away from center.

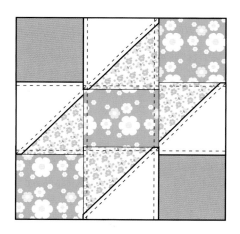

9. Measure and record in box.

12" Finished Block	6" Finished Block
12½" is ideal size	*6½" is ideal size*

It is important that all blocks be one consistent size.

¼" seam allowance

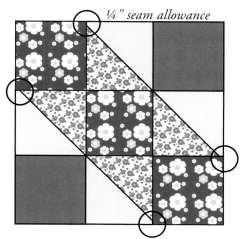

Women's Work

Women workers spent their evenings and spare time mending and restyling clothes, repairing home appliances, stretching their food rationing points, and knitting sweaters. One favorite evening activity was stitching on stamped, ready-to-embroider linens.

Marine Boy Kewpie

Erma Knoechel embroidered "Home, Sweet Home," put out by the Vogart Needlecraft Company. Note their name stamped on the outside edge.

The other two embroidered pieces are tinted pillow covers in patriotic themes. The outside edge of the pillow with the Marine boy kewpie is crocheted. The two sailor dogs are proudly standing on the ship's deck.

Star Spangled Banner

Patriotism was called for across the United States. "Save food for the troops. Plant a Victory Garden." This call was answered by nearly 20 million Americans. These gardens produced up to 40 percent of all the vegetable produce that was consumed in the nation. Mass produced potatoes and carrots were sent overseas to feed the troops.

In Zelienople, Pennsylvania, my mother, Erma Knoechel, did her part planting vegetables including lettuce, tomatoes, green beans, peppers, and zucchini. Toddler Kathy did her part for Victory by helping pull the carrots. Mother had one of the richest gardens around – a herd of cows leisurely grazed nearby, providing her with all the fertilizer she needed.

Skill Level ★

Kansas City Star – 1941

Supplies

12" Block
12½" Square Up Ruler
Fine Point Pen
Template Plastic
Paper Backed Fusible Web
    10" square
Sharp Scissors

6" Block
6½" Triangle Square Up Ruler
Fine Point Pen
Template Plastic
Paper Backed Fusible Web
    6" square
Sharp Scissors

	12" Finished Block	6" Finished Block
Background		
Stripe	(1) 1⅞" x 20" strip	(1) 1⅛" x 11" strip
Light		
Center	(1) 4½" square	(1) 2½" square
Four Stars	(1) 9" square	(1) 4½" square
Medium		
Stripe	(2) 1⅞" x 20" strips	(2) 1¼" x 11" strips
Dark		
Corner Squares	(1) 4½" x 20" strip cut into (4) 4½" squares	(1) 2½" x 11" strip cut into (4) 2½" squares
One Star	(1) 4½" square	(1) 2½" square

Making Stripes

1. Lay out two medium strips and one Background.

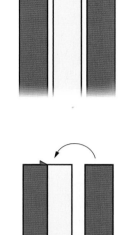

12" Finished Block	6" Finished Block
1⅞" strips	1⅛" and 1¼" strips

2. Flip Backgound strip right sides together to medium strip, and sew with **perfect ¼" seam. Do not sew a scant ¼" seam.**

3. Set seam with medium on top, open, and press toward medium.

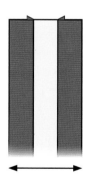

4. Sew remaining medium strip to Background.

5. Set seam with medium on top, open, and press toward medium.

6. Measure. If necessary, sliver trim or resew.

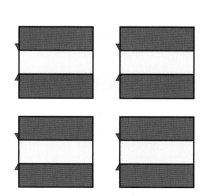

12" Finished Block	6" Finished Block
4½" width	2½" width

7. Cut four squares.

12" Finished Block	6" Finished Block
4½" squares	2½" squares

🔳 **Sewing Block Together**

1. Lay out pieces.

2. Flip middle vertical row to left vertical row, right sides together.

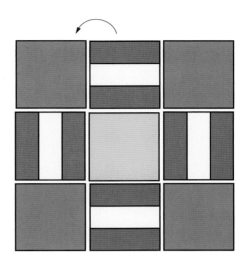

3. Assembly-line sew. Do not clip connecting threads.

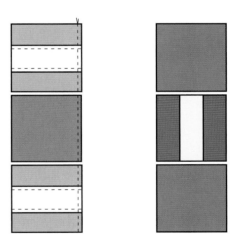

4. Open. Flip right vertical row to middle vertical row, right sides together.

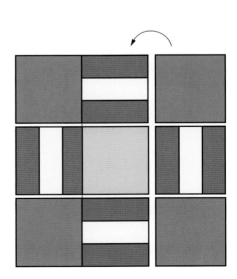

5. Assembly-line sew. Do not clip connecting threads.

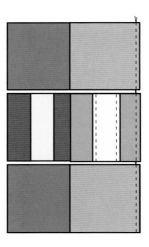

6. Open and turn. Sew remaining rows, locking and pushing seams away from stripes.

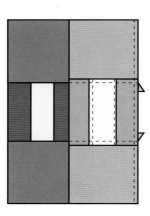

7. Press just sewn seams away from center.

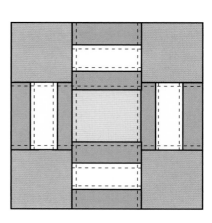

✖ Making Stars

1. Make photocopy of Star pattern, and glue to template plastic. Cut out Star template.

2. Trace five Stars on paper side of paper backed fusible web. Leave ½" between Stars.

3. Rough cut around five Stars with at least ¼" fusible beyond each line.

4. Place dark square **wrong side up** on pressing mat. Center one Star on square with rough fusible side of Star against wrong side of fabric.

12" Finished Block	6" Finished Block
4½" square	2½" square

5. Place light square wrong side up on pressing mat. Place four Stars on square with rough fusible side against wrong side of fabric.

12" Finished Block	6" Finished Block
9" square	4½" square

6. Pre-heat dry iron to silk setting. **Do not use steam.**

7. Place and hold heated iron on paper side of fusible web for **2 seconds**.

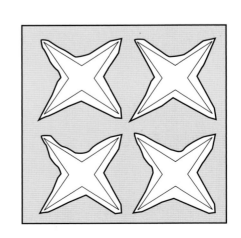

8. Cut out Stars on lines, and then peel off paper backing. Release paper by running thumb nail ¼" from outside edge.

9. Place Stars on squares, allowing ¼" for seams around outside edges. Press in place for **8 – 10** seconds. Check edges to make sure they fused in place.

10. Finish outside raw edges with straight stitch. Stitch into end of point, and pivot with needle down.

11. Measure and record.

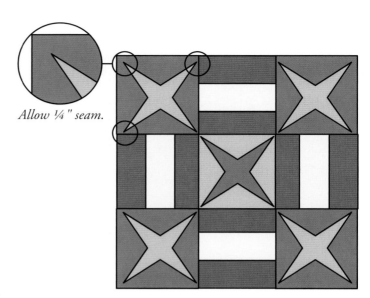

Allow ¼" seam.

12" Finished Block	6" Finished Block

12½" is ideal size   6½" is ideal sizes
It is important that all blocks be one consistent size.

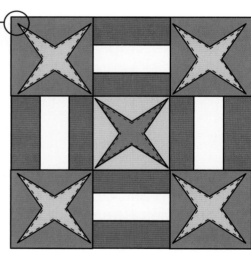

Defense Stamp Album

This Defense Stamp Album was given to Lorna Lenk when she was a baby.

To help pay for the staggering costs of the war, American children could buy stamps for ten cents or more and paste them into a book until they added up to $18.75. In ten years, each book would be worth $25. Practically every school child participated.

Sugarless Cake

During the war with sugar rationing, many versions of sugarless cakes were developed. This particular recipe is one that we can still enjoy.

1 c raisins
1 c dried apricots
1 c dates, chopped
½ c water
2 eggs, beaten

1 stick butter, softened
1 c flour
1 t baking soda
1 t vanilla

In a saucepan, simmer the raisins, apricots, and dates with the water until tender. Cool. Add remaining ingredients and mix well.

Pour into a 9" x 13" baking pan greased with a solid shortening such as Crisco. Bake in preheated 350° oven for 25 minutes. Cool. Serve with Cool Whip or ice cream. Or, dust with powdered sugar.

Comment: Any of a variety of dried fruits can be used. Dried plums, dried apples, and dried pears were often substituted.

Broken Sugar Bowl

The sign of the war's impact was the unprecedented rationing of more than 20 essential items. The first item to be rationed nationwide was sugar, which was soon followed by coffee and shoes. Next came meat, fat, butter, cheese, metal appliances, and gasoline. Women lined up at their local schools, where teachers issued ration books. Once you were out of coupons for a certain product, you could not purchase any more.

A popular slogan during those years was: *"Use it up, wear it out, make it do, or do without."*

It was up to the consumer to be honest and use the coupons and points when purchasing rationed items.

Skill Level ★

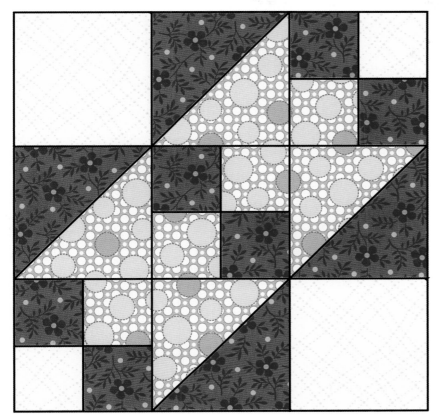

Kansas City Star –1942
The Broken Sugar Bowl
Wallace's Farmer – July 29, 1928
also The Broken Dish

Supplies

 12" Block
6" x 12" Ruler
6½" Triangle Square Up Ruler
12½" Square Up Ruler

6" Block
6" x 12" Ruler
6½" Triangle Square Up Ruler

	12" Finished Block	6" Finished Block
Background		
Four-Patches	(1) 2½" x 6"	(1) 1½" x 4"
Corners	(2) 4½" squares	(2) 2½" squares
Medium		
Four Triangle Pieced Squares	(1) 5" x 10"	(1) 3" x 6"
Four-Patches	(1) 2½" x 11"	(1) 1½" x 7"
Dark		
Four Triangle Pieced Squares	(1) 5" x 10"	(1) 3" x 6"
Four-Patches	(1) 2½" x 6"	(1) 1½" x 4"
Four-Patches	(1) 2½" x 11"	(1) 1½" x 7"

Making Four Triangle Pieced Squares

1. Place medium right sides together to dark.

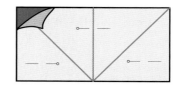

12" Finished Block	6" Finished Block
5" x 10"	3" x 6"

2. Draw a center line.

3. Draw diagonal lines. Pin.

4. Sew a ¼" seam on both sides of diagonal lines. Press.

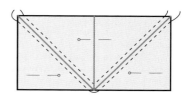

5. Cut apart on drawn lines.

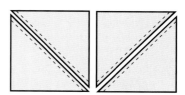

6. Square with 6½" Triangle Square Up Ruler.

12" Finished Block	6" Finished Block
4½" square	2½" square

12" Block

Place 4½" red dashed line on 6½" Triangle Square Up Ruler **above stitching line** to compensate for fold. Center ruler on patch. Trim two sides.

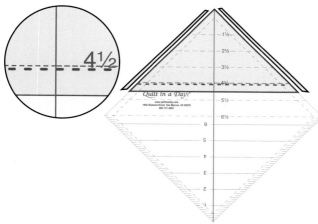

6" Block

Place 2½" red dashed line on 6½" Triangle Square Up Ruler **above stitching line** to compensate for fold. Center ruler on patch. Trim two sides.

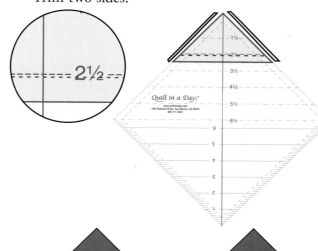

7. Set seam with dark on top.

8. Open, and press seams toward dark.

9. Trim tips.

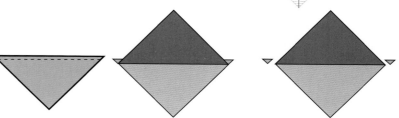

Making Four-Patches

1. Lay out four strips.

12" Finished Block	6" Finished Block
2½" x 6"	1½" x 4"
2½" x 11"	1½" x 7"

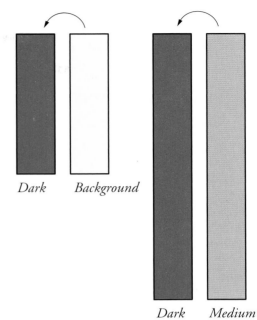

Dark *Background*

Dark *Medium*

2. Flip right sides together, and assembly-line sew.

3. Set seams with **lighter** fabric on top, open, and press toward lighter fabric.

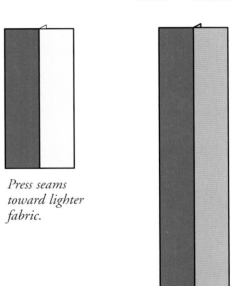

Press seams toward lighter fabric.

4. Place strip sets on cutting mat. Square left end.

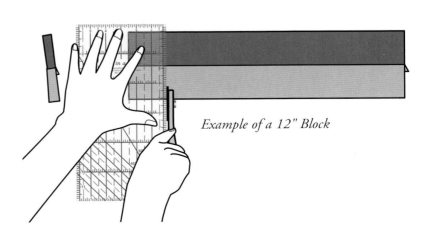

Example of a 12" Block

5. Cut four pieces from medium/dark and two pieces from Background/dark.

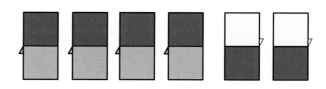

12" Finished Block	6" Finished Block
2½" pieces	1½" pieces

6. Rearrange pieces into Four-Patches.

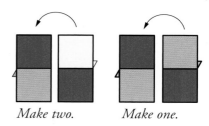

Make two.   *Make one.*

7. Flip right sides together. Lock seams, and assembly-line sew.

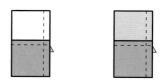

8. Place on pressing mat wrong side up. Push top vertical seam to right, and bottom vertical seam to left. Center will pop open and make a little Four-Patch. Press center flat with your finger.

Push top vertical seam to right.

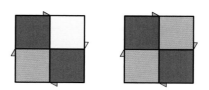

9. Press seams to swirl around center.

Push bottom vertical seam to left.

10. Measure. Trim if too large, or resew if more than ¼" smaller.

12" Finished Block	6" Finished Block
4½" square	2½" square

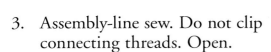 **Sewing Block Together**

1. Lay out pieces.

2. Flip middle vertical row right sides together to left vertical row.

3. Assembly-line sew. Do not clip connecting threads. Open.

4. Flip right vertical row to middle vertical row.

5. Assembly-line sew.

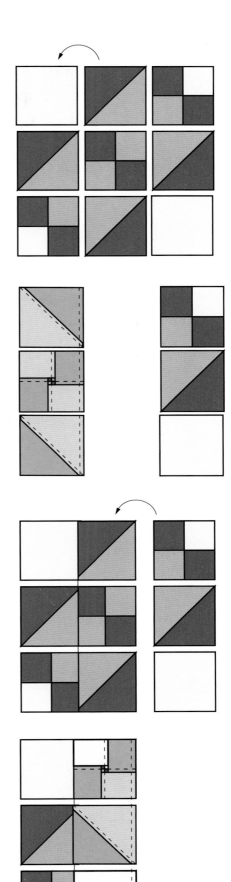

6. Do not clip connecting threads.

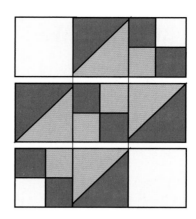

7. Turn block. Flip right vertical row to middle vertical row.

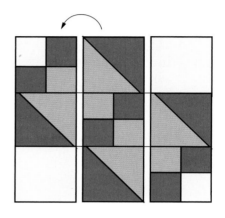

8. Push seams away from triangle pieced squares, lock seams, and sew.

9. Repeat with remaining row.

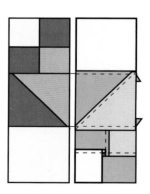

10. Press just sewn seams away from center.

11. Measure and record in box.

12" Finished Block	6" Finished Block
12½" is ideal size	6½" is ideal size

It is important that all blocks be one consistent size.

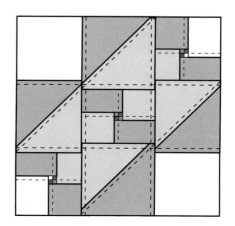

Broken Sugar Bowl Scrappy Quilt

In this variation of Broken Sugar Bowl, each block was made from two Four-Patches and two Triangle Pieced Squares. The quilter made do with the scraps she had on hand. Because it was just a top when discovered recently, perhaps she couldn't afford backing and batting to complete the quilt.

Women had to make do with what was at hand. The motto was "Use it up, wear it out, make it do, or do without." Salvageable parts of clothing and feed sacks were recycled into quilts.

Quilt historians may tell us that quilting was non-existent during World War II. Quilting did not actually disappear; it simply became unimportant in lieu of other pressing events. Women used their piecing as a distraction from worrying about loved ones in battle.

71" x 82"
Quiltmaker Unknown 1940's
Quilted by Judy Jackson 2007

Signal Lights

To keep America safe from enemy bombings, Civil Defense wardens patrolled streets during blackout conditions and air raids. Their job was to keep watch for lights during air raids. They were to also carry messages from one command center to another if communications were knocked out.

Mary Hosie Steutel and her neighbors in Glenhead, New York hung blackout curtains in their windows to ensure total darkness during air raid drills. By day, Mary, a former newspaper reporter and columnist for the Brooklyn Eagle, cared for her young son Brian. By night, when the siren went off, she dutifully walked her neighborhood as an Air Raid Warden, watching for any visible light peaking through her neighbors windows. Over her shoulder was her canvas bag, packed with her issued flashlight and binoculars. The slightest sliver of light would bring her to knock on her neighbor's door.

Normally, the air was filled with the sights and sounds of a big city at night. During an air raid alert, there were no cars, no pedestrians, no radios, or even doors opening and closing, just total silence in near-total darkness. When the "all clear" sounded, the city came back to life.

Mary Hosie Steutel, young mother and newspaper columnist, was an air raid warden in Glenhead, New York.

BLACKOUT POINTERS

Skill Level ★★★

Signal Lights – 1942
Kansas City Star

Supplies

12" Block
Kaleidoscope Ruler and
  Glow-Line™ Tape and
  InvisiGRIP or
Template Plastic
6½" Fussy Cut Ruler
12½" Square Up Ruler

6" Block
Kaleidoscope Ruler and
  Glow-Line™ Tape and
  InvisiGRIP or
Template Plastic
3½" Fussy Cut Ruler
6½" Fussy Cut Ruler

	12" Finished Block	6" Finished Block
Background		
Side Triangles	(2) 3¼" x 7¾"	(2) 2" x 4¾"
Light		
Side Triangles	(2) 3¼" x 7¾"	(2) 2" x 4¾"
Light Medium		
Four Triangles	(1) 3½" x 9"	(1) 2" x 7"
Dark Medium		
Center Square	(1) 5¼" square	(1) 2⅞" square
Dark		
Twelve Triangles	(2) 3½" x 13"	(2) 2" x 9"

◬ Making a Triangle Template

1. Make photocopy of template, and glue to template plastic.

2. Carefully cut out on lines with ruler and rotary cutter.

Or Using a Kaleidoscope Ruler

1. Put InvisiGRIP™ on back side of ruler so ruler does not slide while cutting triangles.

2. Put a piece of Glow-Line™ tape on designated measurement.

12" Block

6" Block

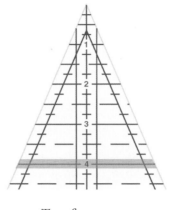
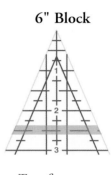

12" Finished Block	6" Finished Block
3⅞" line	2⅜" line

Top of tape at 3⅞" ruler line

Top of tape at 2⅜" ruler line

3. Layer one strip for Four Light Medium Triangles and two strips for Twelve Dark Triangles right side up.

12" Finished Block	6" Finished Block
3½" x 9"	2" x 7"
3½" x 13"	2" x 9"

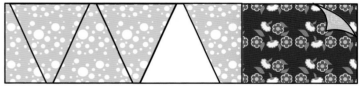

Template Plastic: *Trace and cut on lines with ruler and rotary cutter.*

4. Place template or ruler on left end. **Triangles have blunt tops.**

5. Mark and/or cut four medium triangles. Remove excess medium fabric, and continue cutting a total of twelve dark triangles.

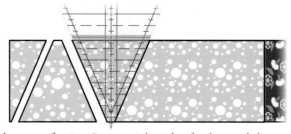

Kaleidoscope Ruler: *Place designated line against bottom of strip. Cut up right side of ruler, and down left side. Turn ruler upside down, and place designated line across top of strip. Continue cutting.*

▲ Sewing Pieced Triangles

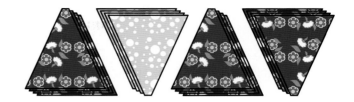

1. Lay out three stacks of dark and one stack of light medium triangles. Place four in each stack.

2. Select one stack of dark and one stack of light medium. Flip light medium triangle right sides together to dark triangle on left.

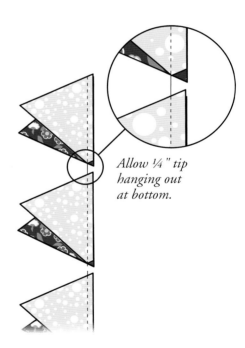

3. **Line up bottom edge first** with ¼" dark tip hanging out. Line up sides.

4. Assembly-line sew. Clip connecting threads.

Allow ¼" tip hanging out at bottom.

5. Set seam with dark triangle on top.

6. Open, and press seam toward dark.

7. Place second stack of four dark triangles to right of patch.

8. Flip right sides together. Line up top edge with ¼" medium tip hanging over.

9. Assembly-line sew.

10. Set seam with dark triangle on top.

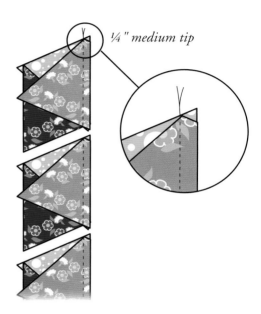

¼ " medium tip

11. Open, and press toward dark.

12. Place third stack of four dark triangles to right of patch.

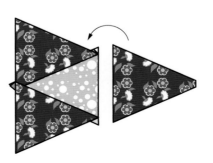

13. Flip right sides together. Line up dark tips on sides with medium tips.

14. Assembly-line sew.

15. Set seam with dark triangle on top.

16. Open, and carefully press toward dark.

17. Carefully trim sides of triangles without trimming away ¼" seam.

◭ Sewing Side Triangles

1. Place pair of Light rectangles wrong side together.

2. Place pair of Background rectangles wrong side together.

12" Finished Block	6" Finished Block
3¼" x 7¾"	2" x 4¾"

3. Cut pairs on diagonal.

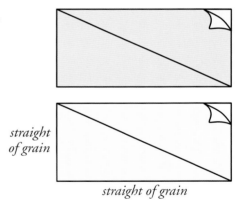

straight of grain

straight of grain

4. Stack both sets of Side Triangles right side up. Place with straight of grain on outside edges.

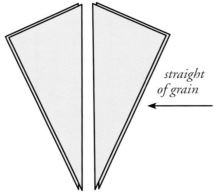

straight of grain

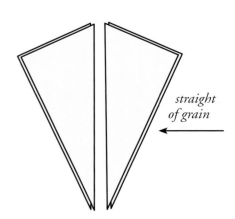

straight of grain

5. Split Side Triangles apart, and place two Pieced Triangles between each set.

6. Flip Side Triangle onto Pieced Triangle.

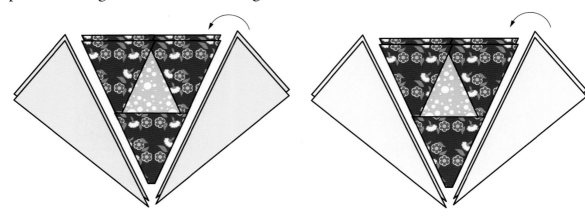

7. Line up straight edges at top. Assembly-line sew. Carefully sew narrow part of tips. Use stiletto to help guide pieces.

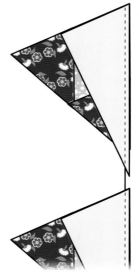

Line up straight edges at top.

8. Set seam with Side Triangle on top, open, and press toward Side Triangle. Carefully press tip so there is not a fold in the seam.

9. Trim tip even with side of triangle.

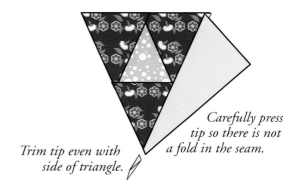

Trim tip even with side of triangle.

Carefully press tip so there is not a fold in the seam.

10. Place Pieced Triangle patch beside left Side Triangle.

11. Flip patch onto left Triangle.

12. Line up straight edges at top. Assembly-line sew.

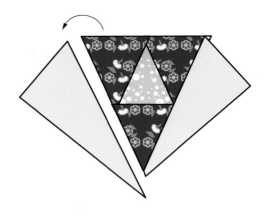

13. Set seam with Side Triangle on top, open, and press toward Side Triangle.

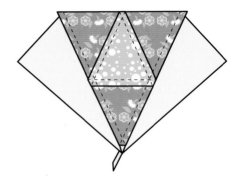

14. Square up with Fussy Cut Ruler. Leave ¼" seam allowance at top. Line up diagonal line on ruler with triangles. Trim on all four sides.

12" Finished Block	6" Finished Block
6½" square	3½" square

Leave ¼" seam allowance at top.

Trim to corners.

15. Check seams on back side.

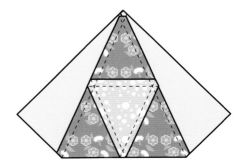

✳ Sewing Triangles to Center Square

1. Lay out four triangles with Center Square.

12" Finished Block	6" Finished Block
5¼" square	2⅞" square

2. Flip one triangle right sides together to Center Square. Pin layers together ¼" from outside edges.

3. Sew from triangle side. Start and stop ¼" from outside edges. **Do not press.** Open.

Start and stop ¼" from outside edges.

4. Repeat on opposite side with matching patch. Open. **Do not press.**

5. Fold first two triangles away from Center. Place third triangle. Flip right side together. Pin ¼" from ends and sew.

6. Repeat with fourth triangle.

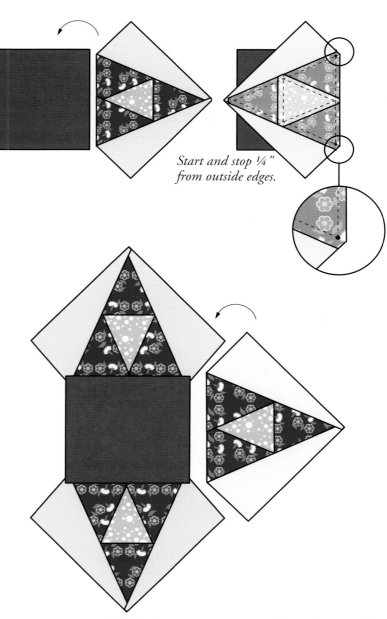

Sewing Side Seams

1. Swing one set of Side seams right sides together. Pull pieced Triangle seams out of way. Pin ¼" from outside edges. Sew from Center square to edge.

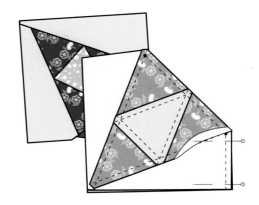

2. Repeat with remaining three sides.

3. Press side seams to light side, and press middle seams toward Center Square.

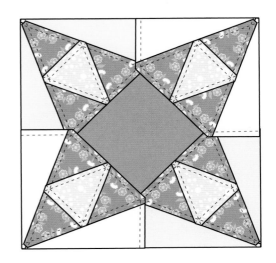

4. Measure and record in box.

12" Finished Block	6" Finished Block
12½" is ideal size	*6½" is ideal size*

It is important that all blocks be one consistent size.

Stars and Stripes

Young Patriots helped on the home front to win the war. Girl Scouts collected silk and nylon hose to be recycled for parachutes and gunpowder bags. Little "scavengers" searched trash for gum wrappers and cigarette packs to retrieve the silver. Neighborhood theatres held "aluminum matinees" where each child with an aluminum item was admitted free to the matinee. Chirldren helped mothers and grandmothers serve coffee and doughnuts to troops as they boarded ships for overseas duty. The ultimate sacrifice some gave was losing a parent!

Skill Level ★

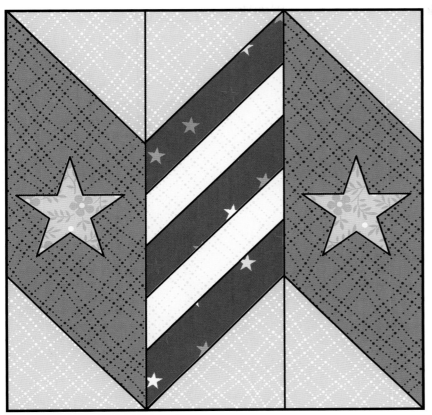

Stars and Stripes, Nancy Cabot

Supplies

12" Block
6" x 24" Ruler
6½" Triangle Square Up Ruler
12½" Square Up Ruler
Template plastic
Paper Backed Fusible Web 3" x 6"

6" Block
6" x 12" Ruler
6½" Triangle Square Up Ruler
Template plastic
Paper Backed Fusible Web 2" x 4"

	12" Finished Block	6" Finished Block
Background		
Stripe	(2) 1¾" x 10"	(2) 1⅛" x 6"
Light		
Corners	(1) 5" square	(1) 3" square
	(1) 4½" x 19" cut into	(1) 2½" x 11" cut into
	(4) 4½" squares	(4) 2½" squares
Light Medium		
Stars	(1) 4" x 9"	(1) 1½" x 3"
Dark Medium		
Stripe	(3) 1¾" x 10"	(3) 1⅛" x 6"
Dark		
Rectangles	(2) 4½" x 12½"	(2) 2½" x 6½"

Sewing Rows One and Three

1. Turn four light squares for Corners wrong sides up. Draw diagonal lines from corner to corner.

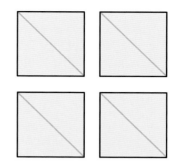

12" Finished Block	6" Finished Block
4½" squares	2½" squares

2. Place marked square on each end of two dark rectangles.

12" Finished Block	6" Finished Block
4½" x 12½"	2½" x 6½"

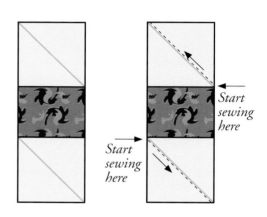

3. Place open toe foot on your sewing machine. Sew on outside edge of diagonal line.

   It's easier if you start in middle and sew to corner so fabric doesn't get eaten up in throat plate's hole.

4. Trim ¼" from diagonal line.

5. **Press seams toward dark.**

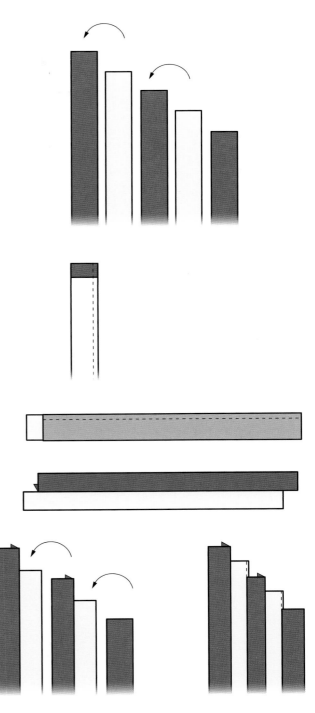

Sewing Row Two Together

1. Lay out three dark medium and two Background strips in alternating order, beginning with medium. Place each strip 1" lower than previous strip.

12" Finished Block	6" Finished Block
1¾" x 10" Background	1⅛" x 6" Backgound
1¾" x 10" dark medium	1⅛" x 6" dark medium

2. Flip Background right sides together to dark medium and assembly-line sew with ¼" seam.
   Do not sew with a scant ¼" seam.

3. Set seam with dark medium on top, open, and press toward dark medium.

4. Sew five strips together.
5. Set seam with medium on top, open and press toward medium.

6. Measure width. **Sliver trim if wider, or resew if too narrow.**

12" Finished Block

6" Finished Block

6¼"

3⅜"

125

7. Turn Quilt in a Day's 6" x 12" Ruler upside down.

8. Line up 45° line on 6" x 12" Ruler across top of Stripes, and cut **on right side only.**

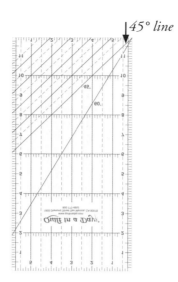

45° line

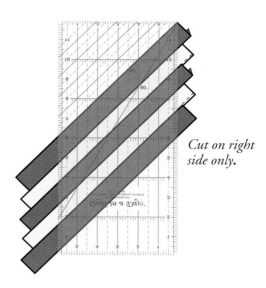

Cut on right side only.

9. Turn ruler right side up. Turn patch. Cut remainder of Stripe into a section.

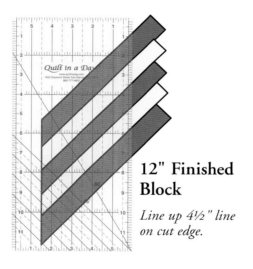

12" Finished Block

Line up 4½" line on cut edge.

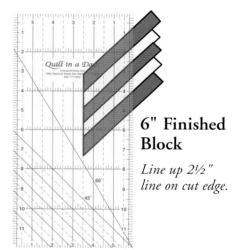

6" Finished Block

Line up 2½" line on cut edge.

10. Cut one light Corner square in half on diagonal into two triangles.

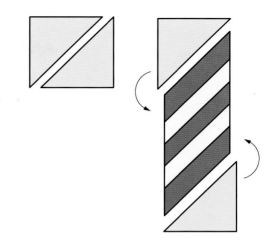

12" Finished Block	6" Finished Block
5" square	3" square

11. Place light triangles with Stripe.

12. Flip right sides together.

13. Line up edge of triangle with strips, and sew.

14. Press seams toward triangles.

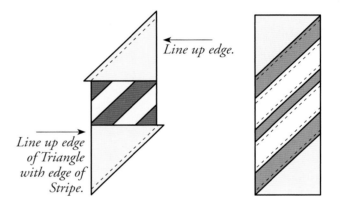

Line up edge.

Line up edge of Triangle with edge of Stripe.

15. Place ruler on Stripe. Trim two long sides, turn ruler, and trim tips from top and bottom.

12" Finished Block	6" Finished Block
4½" x 12½"	2½" x 6½"

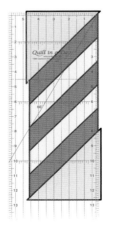

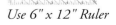

Use 6" x 12" Ruler

Use 6" x 24" Ruler

Sewing Block Together

1. Lay out three rows.

2. Flip Row Two right sides together to Row One.

3. Lock seams, and pin.

4. Sew with ¼" seam, pulling out pins just before sewing over locked seams.

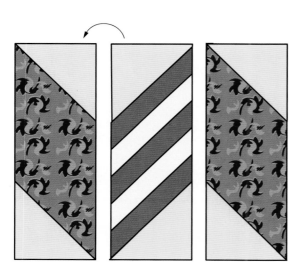
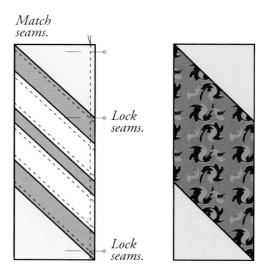

5. Open. Flip Row Three to Row Two. Lock seams, pin, and sew.

6. Press just sewn seams away from center.

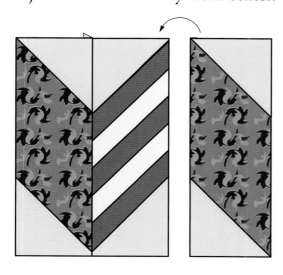
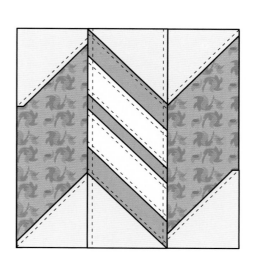

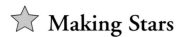 **Making Stars**

1. Photocopy Stars, glue to template plastic, and cut out.

12" Finished Block	6" Finished Block
3" x 6"	2" x 4"

2. Trace two Stars on paper side of paper-backed fusible web. Rough cut around Stars.

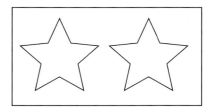

3. Place light medium Fabric wrong side up on pressing mat. Center Stars with rough fusible side of Stars against wrong side of fabric.

4. Pre-heat dry iron to silk setting. **Do not use steam.**

5. Place and hold heated iron on paper side of fusible web for **2 seconds.**

6. Cut out Stars on lines, and peel off paper backing.

7. Center Stars on Rows One and Three, allowing ¼" for outside seams.

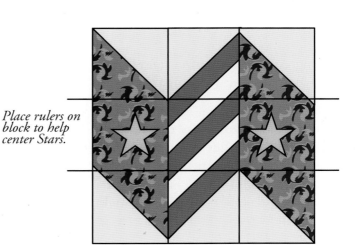

Place rulers on block to help center Stars.

8. Press in place for **8 – 10** seconds. Check edges to make sure they fused in place.

9. Finish outside raw edges with straight stitch.

10. Measure and record in box. Square up if necessary.

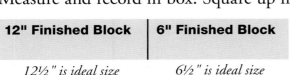

12" Finished Block	6" Finished Block
12½" is ideal size	*6½" is ideal size*

It is important that all blocks be one consistent size.

Service Flag

The Service Flag is an official banner that the family of service members in harm's way can display. The banner has a white background and red border, with a blue star for each family member in active duty. If a family member dies during service, a smaller gold star is sewn on top of the blue star, with the blue edge showing. It's also called the Blue Star Service Banner, or a Gold Star Service Banner. Flags can feature up to five stars.

Banners became extremely popular during World War II, and were hung in windows of service member's homes.

Shortly after World War I, the Gold Star Mothers Club was formed to provide support of mothers who lost sons or daughters in the war. They continue volunteer work together, and serve as a support network for one another. Gold Star Mother's Day is observed in the United States in their honor on the last Sunday in September.

In 1942, the Blue Star Mothers of America was founded to provide care packages to military members serving overseas. They also provide assistance to families who encountered hardships during the war. Silver Star Families organization is encouraging the U. S. Congress to make a silver star official for those wounded in military service.

During World War I, Army Capt. Robert L. Queissner had two sons serving on the front line. He created and patented the white background, red border and one or more blue stars in the center design, but turned the rights to the flag over to the U. S. Government once it became popular. Current manufacture of these flags are only by specific government license.

84" x 112"

Pieced by Heidi McFadden
Applique by Betty Adams
Quilted by Susie Johnson

Heidi McFadden and her team of assistants made this beautiful patriotic quilt following directions found on www.militarymoms.net/bsbquilt.html. Credit was given to the American legion for granting permission to use the blue star banner in designing this quilt.

The team made the quilt as a fundraiser for wives and children of their Marine squadron, HMH-466. They auctioned it off on ebay, and raised a whooping $2,550, all of which will go back to the families at the squadron's

Army Star

World War II was the largest and most violent armed conflict in the history of mankind. However, it united us as people with a common purpose.

Over 150,000 American women served in the Women's Army Corps (WAC) during World War 11. Members of the WAC were the first women other than nurses to serve within the ranks of the United States Army. Both the Army and the American public initially had difficulty accepting the concept of women in uniform. By the end of the war their contributions were widely praised.

PFC George Voigtlander, father of Merritt Voigtlander, Art Director at Quilt in a Day, served in the Pacific.

Cpl Erwin Knoechel and a buddy in Weis-baden, Germany

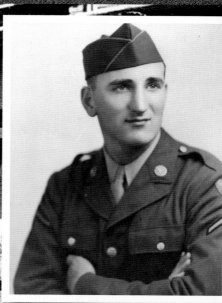

Corporal Erwin Knoechel, father of Eleanor Burns, served in Germany.

Skill Level ★ ★

Kansas City Star – 1941

Supplies

12" Block
Mini Geese Ruler Two
   (Finished Size 1½" x 3")
6" x 24" Ruler
6½" Triangle Square Up Ruler
12½" Square Up Ruler

6" Block
Mini Geese Ruler Two
   (Finished Size ¾" x 1½")
6" x 12" Ruler
6½" Triangle Square Up Ruler

	12" Finished Block	6" Finished Block
Background		
Wide Stripe	(1) 3½" x 15"	(1) 2" x 9"
Light		
Four Little Squares	(1) 2" x 9" cut into (4) 2" squares	(1) 1¼" x 6" cut into (4) 1¼" squares
Four Triangle Pieced Squares	(1) 4" x 8"	(1) 2½" x 5"
Light Medium		
Four Triangle Pieced Squares	(1) 4" x 8"	(1) 2½" x 5"
Dark Medium		
Star Points	(1) 4½" square	(1) 3" square
Stripes	(2) 2" x 15"	(2) 1¼" x 9"
Dark		
Star Points	(1) 6" square	(1) 4½" square
Center Square	(1) 3½" square	(1) 2" square

Making Star Points

Star Points are made with a patch called Geese Patch. One set of squares makes four Star Points.

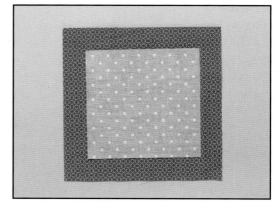

1. Place smaller Star Points square right sides together and centered on larger Star Points square. Press.

12" Finished Block	6" Finished Block
4½" square	3" square
6" square	4½" square

2. Place ruler on squares so ruler touches all four corners. Draw diagonal line across squares.

3. Pin squares together. Sew ¼" on both sides of drawn line. Use 15 stitches per inch or 2.0 on computerized machines. Remove pins.

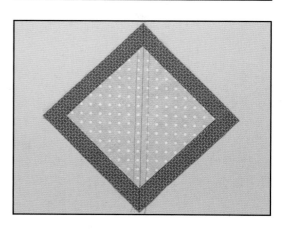

4. Cut on drawn line.

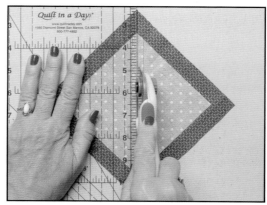

5. Place on pressing mat with large triangle on top. Press to set seam.

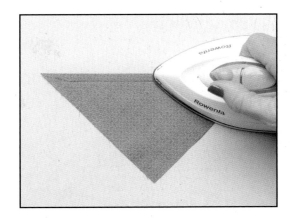

6. Open and press flat. Check that there are no tucks, and seam is pressed toward larger triangle.

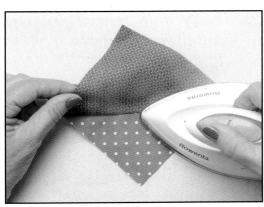

7. Place pieces right sides together so that opposite fabrics touch. **Seams are parallel with each other.**

8. Match outside edges. There is a gap between seams. **The seams do not lock.**

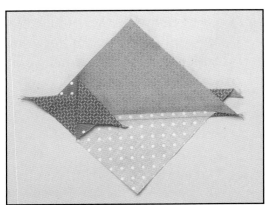

9. Draw a diagonal line across seams. Pin.

10. Sew ¼" from both sides of drawn line. Hold seams flat with stiletto so seams do not flip. Press to set seam.

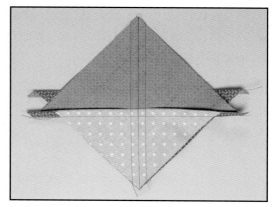

11. Cut on drawn line.

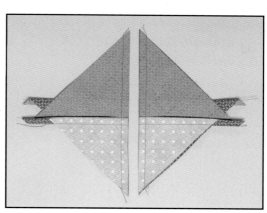

12. Fold in half. Clip seam allowance to vertical seam midway between horizontal seam. This allows the seam allowance to be pressed toward Star Points.

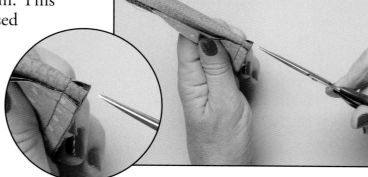

13. From right side, press into one Star Point. Turn and press into second Star Point.

14. Turn over, and press on wrong side. At clipped seam, fabric is pressed toward Star Points.

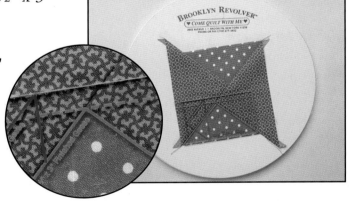

Squaring Up 12" Block with Mini Geese Ruler Two

1. Place InvisiGRIP™ on bottom side of 1½" x 3" Mini Flying Geese Ruler Two.

2. Place patch on small cutting mat so you can rotate mat as you cut. Place 1½" x 3" Mini Ruler on patch. **Line up ruler's green solid lines on sewn lines for 1½" x 3" Finished Geese.** Line up green dotted line with peak of triangle

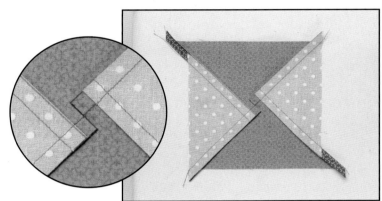

3. Hold ruler securely on fabric. Cut block in half, and separate two patches.

4. Trim off excess fabric on right.

5. Turn mat. Trim off excess fabric on right and top. **Patch should measure 2" x 3½".**

6. Repeat with remaining half.

Patch should measure 2" x 3½".

Squaring Up 6" Block with Mini Geese Ruler Two

1. Place InvisiGRIP™ on bottom side of 1½" x 3" Mini Flying Geese Ruler Two.

2. Place patch on small cutting mat right side up. Place Mini Ruler in vertical position on patch. **Line up ruler's red solid lines on sewn lines for ¾" x 1½" Finished Geese.** Line up red dotted line with peak of triangle for ¼" seam.

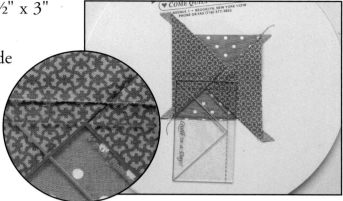

3. Hold ruler securely on fabric so it doesn't shift while cutting.

4. Cut block in half, and separate two patches.

5. Trim off excess fabric on right.

6. Turn patch. Do not turn mat. Trim off excess fabric on right and top. **Patch should measure 1¼" x 2".**

Patch should measure 1¼" x 2".

7. Repeat with remaining half.

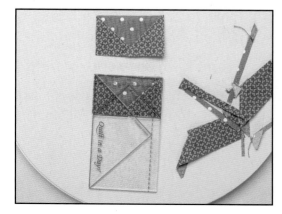

✦ Making Center Star

1. Lay out the Center Square, Little Squares and Star Points.

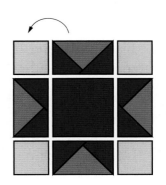

12" Finished Block	6" Finished Block
2" x 3½" Points	1¼" x 2" Points
3½" Center Square	2" Center Square
2" Little Squares	1¼" Little Squares

2. Flip middle vertical row to left vertical row. Assembly-line sew. Do not clip connecting threads.

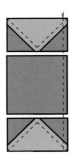

3. Open and add right vertical row.

4. Turn. Sew first horizontal row, pressing seams toward Star Center, and away from Star Points.

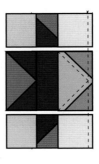
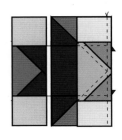

5. Sew second horizontal row, repeating seams. Set seams, open, and press.

6. Check from wrong side. Horizontal seams should be pressed away from center. Measure your block.

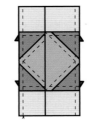
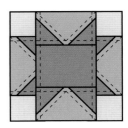

12" Finished Block	6" Finished Block
6½" square	3½" square

▨ Making Four Corner Triangle Pieced Squares

1. Place light and light medium rectangles right sides together with light on top.

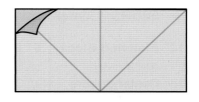

12" Finished Block	6" Finished Block
4" x 8"	2½" x 5"

2. Draw center line.

3. Draw diagonal lines. Pin.

4. Sew a ¼" seam on both sides of diagonal lines. Set seam.

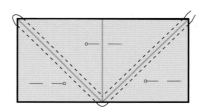

5. Cut apart on drawn lines.

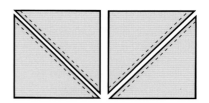

6. Square with 6½" Triangle Square Up Ruler.

12" Finished Block	6" Finished Block
3½" square	2" square

12" Finished Block

Place 3½" red dashed line on 6½" Triangle Square Up Ruler **above stitching line to compensate for fold**. Center ruler on patch. Trim two sides.

6" Finished Block

Place 2" solid green line on 6½" Triangle Square Up Ruler **above stitching line to compensate for fold**. Center ruler on patch. Trim two sides.

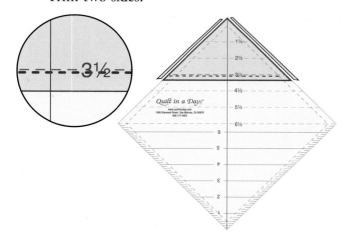

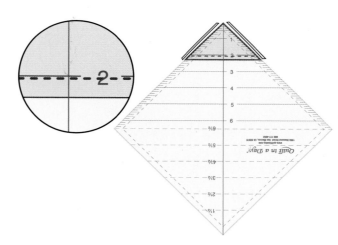

7. Set seam with medium on top.

8. Open, and press seams toward light medium.

9. Trim tips.

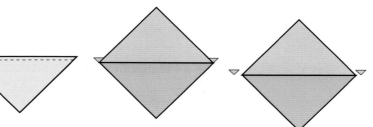

Sewing Stripes Together

1. Lay out one Background and two dark medium stripes and sew together.

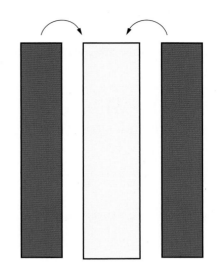

12" Finished Block	6" Finished Block
3½" x 15"	2" x 9"
2" x 15"	1¼" x 9"

2. Press **seams toward Background** so seams lock together.

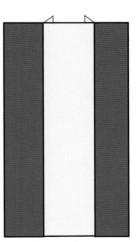

Press seams toward Background.

3. Square left end. Cut into four pieces.

12" Finished Block	6" Finished Block
3½" pieces	2" pieces

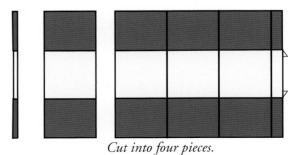

Cut into four pieces.

✳ **Sewing Block Together**

1. Lay out Corners, Stripes, and Center Star.

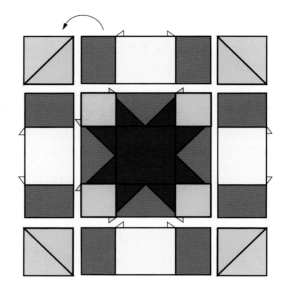

2. Flip middle vertical row to left vertical row, right sides together.

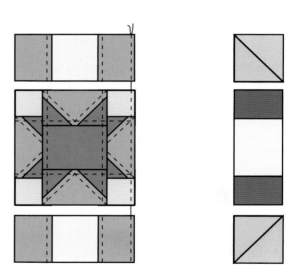

3. Assembly-line sew. Do not clip connecting threads. Open.

4. Flip right vertical row to middle vertical row right sides together, and assembly-line sew. Do not clip connecting threads.

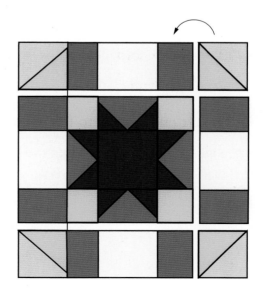

5. Turn. Sew remaining rows, pushing seams away from Corner Squares and Star Corners, locking seams.

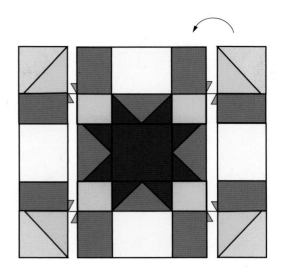

6. Press just sewn seams away from center.

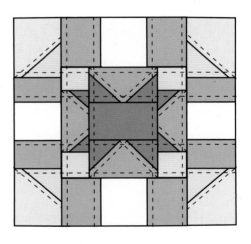

7. Measure and record in box.

12" Finished Block	6" Finished Block
12½" is ideal size	*6½" is ideal size*

It is important that all blocks be one consistent size.

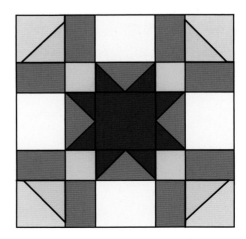

Propeller

Six million women worked in the manufacturing plants that produced munitions and material during World War. These women took the places of male workers who were absent fighting in the Pacific and Europe.

Some women started working without the benefit of formal training programs. Others learned how to do their jobs by educating themselves. They were schoolteachers, artists, and housewives. They loved the challenge of getting dirty, and took pride in what they did!

Regardless of how well trained they were, women war workers had to overcome many obstacles. Working conditions were difficult. Plants extremely dirty with oil on the floor, the work area was very crowded, and the noise level was high. Factory work was also frequently dangerous, and women workers were injured, disabled, and even killed in industrial accidents.

Skill Level ★

Propeller – 1943
Broken Arrows, Quilt World October – 1979

Supplies

12" Block
6" Square Up Ruler
6½" Triangle Square Up Ruler
12½" Square Up Ruler

6" Block
6" Square Up Ruler
6½" Triangle Square Up Ruler
9½" Square Up Ruler

	12" Finished Block	6" Finished Block
Background		
Center Square	(1) 2⅞" square	(1) 1¾" square
Center Strip	(1) 2⅞" x 13"	(1) 1¾" x 8"
Light		
Corners	(1) 6" x 12"	(1) 3½" x 7"
Medium		
Corners	(1) 6" x 12"	(1) 3½" x 7"
Dark		
Center Strip	(1) 2⅞" x 13"	(1) 1¾" x 8"

Making Four Corners

1. Place light and medium Corner rectangles right sides together with light on top.

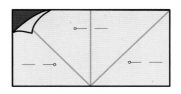

12" Finished Block	6" Finished Block
6" x 12"	3½" x 7"

2. Draw a center line.

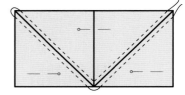

3. Draw diagonal lines. Pin.

4. Sew a ¼" seam on both sides of diagonal lines. Press.

5. Cut apart on drawn lines.

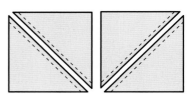

6. Square with 6½" Triangle Square Up Ruler. Place ruler with solid green lines on top. **Notice ⅛" marks drawn along outside edges.**

12" Finished Block	6" Finished Block
5¼" squares	2⅞" squares

12" Finished Block
Place 5¼" **solid red line on outside edges of ruler** slightly above horizontal stitching line to compensate for fold. Trim two sides.

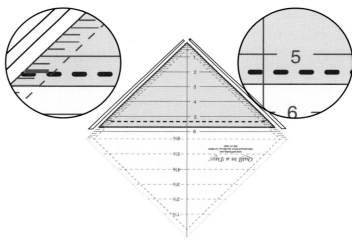

6" Finished Block

Place 2⅞" **solid green lines on outside edges of ruler** slightly above horizontal stitching line to compensate for fold. Trim two sides.

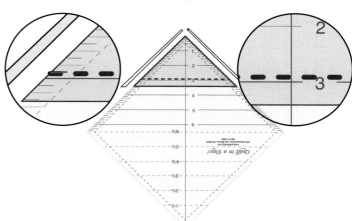

7. Set seam with medium on top. Open and press toward medium. Trim tips.

Making Center Strips

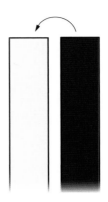

1. Lay out dark and Background Center Strips.

12" Finished Block	6" Finished Block
2⅞" x 13"	1¾" x 8"

2. Flip right sides together, and sew.

3. Set seam with dark on top. Open, and press seam toward dark.

4. **Measure. Sliver trim Background if necessary.**

12" Finished Block	6" Finished Block
5¼" wide	2⅞" wide

Measure. Sliver trim Background if necessary.

5. Cut into four pieces.

12" Finished Block	6" Finished Block
2⅞" pieces	1¾" pieces

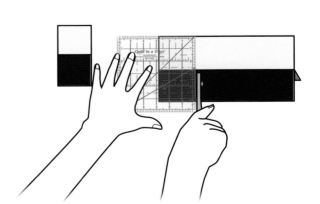

Sewing Block Together

1. Lay out Center Strips, Corners, and Center square.

12" Finished Block	6" Finished Block
2⅞" Center square	1¾" Center square

2. Flip middle vertical row right sides together to left vertical row.

3. Assembly-line sew. Do not clip connecting threads.

4. Open.

5. Flip right vertical row to middle vertical row.

6. Assembly-line sew. Do not clip connecting threads. Open.

Do not clip connecting threads.

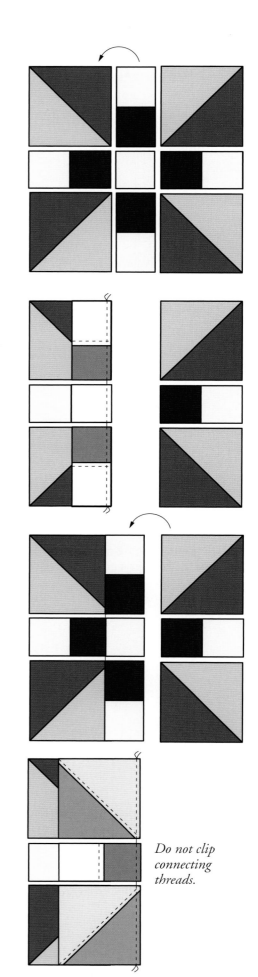

7. From wrong side, press side seams toward Center strips. In center row, press seams away from Center square.

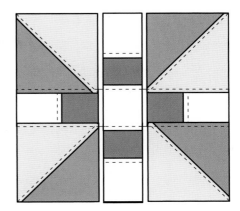

8. Sew remaining rows, locking seams.

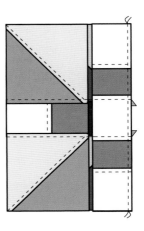

9. Press seams toward center.

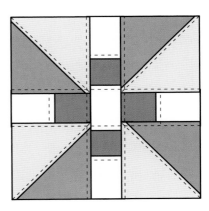

10. Measure and record in box.

12" Finished Block	6" Finished Block
12½ " is ideal size	*6½ " is ideal size*

It is important that all blocks be one consistent size.

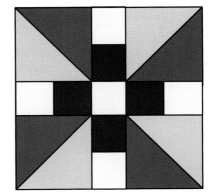

Airplane

American pilot trainee Shirley Slade (1921 - 2000), in uniform, at Avanger Field, Sweetwater, Texas.

(Photo by Peter Stackpole/Time & Life Pictures/Getty Images)

During World War II, a select group of young women pilots became pioneers, heroes, and role models. They were the Women Airforce Service Pilots, WASP, the first women in history trained to fly American military aircraft.

Jean Pearson, pilot trainee in Women's Flying Training Detachment to later join the all-civilian Women's Auxiliary Ferrying Squadron, using a beret and a ribbon-tied hair knot to keep hair from flying, in cockpit of trainer before takeoff at Avenger Field.

In less than 2 years, WASP flew 60 million miles in every type aircraft in the Army Air Force arsenal–from fighters to the heaviest bombers.

They flew every type mission any Army Air Force male pilot flew during World War II, except combat.

They are role models for today's female pilots and astronauts.

(Photo by Peter Stackpole/Time & Life Pictures/Getty Images)

Skill Level ★★

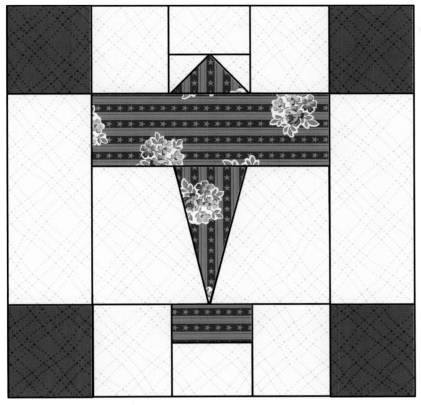

The Aircraft Quilt, Kansas City Star – 1929
Aeroplane, Oklahoma Farmer Stockman – 1929
Airplane, Carrie Hall

Supplies

12" Block
Template Plastic
4" x 14" Ruler
6" Square Up Ruler

6" Block
Template Plastic
4" x 14" Ruler
6" Square Up Ruler

	12" Finished Block	**6" Finished Block**
Background		
Nose	(2) 1¾" squares	(2) 1⅛" squares
Nose Top	(1) 1¾" x 3"	(1) 1⅛" x 1¾"
Nose Sides	(2) 2¾" x 3"	(2) 1¾" squares
Left and Right Fuselage	(2) 4⅛" x 5¼"	(2) 2½" x 3½"
Tail Bottom	(1) 2" x 3"	(1) 1¼" x 1¾"
Tail Sides	(2) 2¾" x 3"	(2) 1¾" squares
Airplane Sides	(2) 3" x 7½"	(2) 1¾" x 4⅛"
Medium		
Nose	(1) 1¾" x 3"	(1) 1⅛" x 1¾"
Wings	(1) 2¾" x 7½"	(1) 1¾" x 4⅛"
Fuselage	(1) 3½" x 6"	(1) 2½" x 3½"
Tail	(1) 1½" x 3"	(1) 1" x 1¾"
Dark		
Corners	(1) 3" x 13" strip cut into (4) 3" squares	(1) 1¾" x 9" strip cut into (4) 1¾" squares

Making Nose

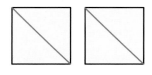

1. Turn two Background squares wrong sides up. Draw diagonal lines.

12" Finished Block	6" Finished Block
1¾" squares	1⅛" squares

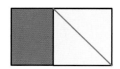

2. Place one Background square right sides together to right corner of medium Nose rectangle.

12" Finished Block	6" Finished Block
1¾" x 3"	1⅛" x 1¾"

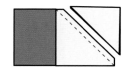

3. Place open toe applique foot on sewing machine. Sew on diagonal line.

4. Trim ¼" away from line.

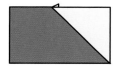

5. Set seam, open, and press toward Background.

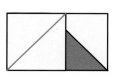

6. Place remaining Background square on left side of Nose rectangle.

7. Sew on diagonal line.

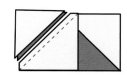

8. Trim ¼" away.

9. Set seam, open, and press toward Background.

10. Measure. Trim if larger without trimming away seam allowance or resew if smaller.

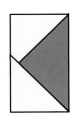

12" Finished Block	6" Finished Block
1¾" x 3"	1⅛" x 1¾"

11. Sew Nose Top to Nose.

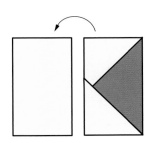

12" Finished Block	6" Finished Block
1¾" x 3"	1⅛" x 1¾"

12. Set seam with Background on top, open, and press toward Background.

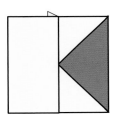

13. Sew Nose Sides to Nose. Set seams with Background on top, open, and press toward Background.

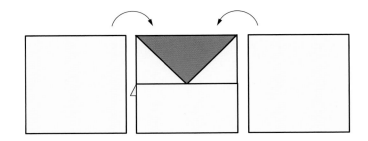

12" Finished Block	6" Finished Block
2¾" x 3"	1¾" squares

14. Measure. Trim if larger without trimming away seam allowance.

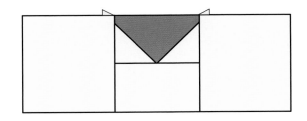

12" Finished Block	6" Finished Block
3" x 7½"	1¾" x 4⅛"

Adding Wings

1. Sew Wings to Nose.

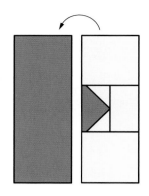

12" Finished Block	6" Finished Block
2¾" x 7½"	1¾" x 4⅛"

2. Set seam with Wings on top, open, and press toward Wings.

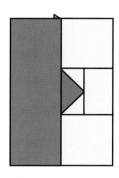

 Sewing the Fuselage

1. Make photocopy of Fuselage template. Glue to template plastic and cut out.

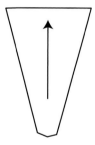

2. Trace Fuselage on wrong side of fabric and cut out.

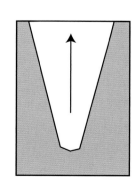 

12" Finished Block	6" Finished Block
3½" x 6"	2½" x 3½"

3. Place pair of Background Fuselage rectangles **wrong sides together**.

12" Finished Block	6" Finished Block
4⅛" x 5¼"	2½" x 3½"

4. Place mark across top of rectangles from right edge.

12" Finished Block	6" Finished Block
1⅜" Mark	⅞" Mark

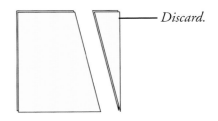

1⅜ "

Example of 12" Block at 1⅜ " mark

5. Layer cut from mark to corner. Discard triangles.

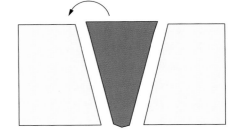

— Discard.

6. Lay out two trimmed Background rectangles with dark triangle for Fuselage.

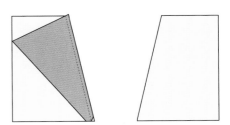

7. Flip Fuselage right sides together to Background on left. Line up two pieces on bottom edge. Let Fuselage hang over ¼" on top. Sew with ¼" seam.

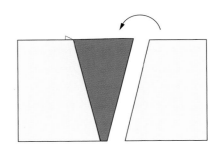

8. Set seam with Background on top, open, and press toward Background.

9. Flip remaining Background right sides together to Fuselage. Let Body hang over ¼" on top, and Background hang over ⅛" on bottom. Sew.

10. Press seam toward Background.

11. Measure. Square up Fuselage without trimming away bottom seam allowance.

12" Finished Block	6" Finished Block
5¼" x 7½"	2⅞" x 4⅛"

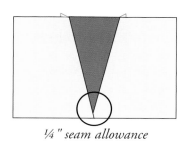

¼ " seam allowance

12. Center Fuselage under Wings. Flip right sides together, and sew.

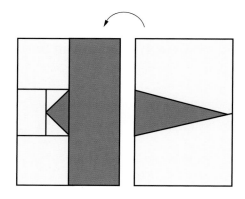

13. Press seam toward Wing. If necessary, straighten sides.

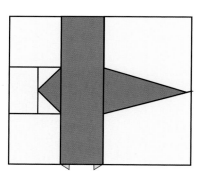

14. Check from back side.

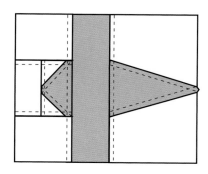

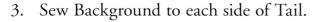 **Sewing the Tail**

1. Lay out Tail Bottom from Background with medium Tail. Flip right sides together, and sew.

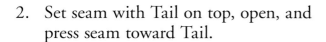

12" Finished Block	6" Finished Block
2" x 3" Background	1¼" x 1¾" Background
1½" x 3" Tail	1" x 1¾" Tail

2. Set seam with Tail on top, open, and press seam toward Tail.

3. Sew Background to each side of Tail.

12" Finished Block	6" Finished Block
2¾" x 3"	1¾" squares

4. Set seam with Background on top, open and press toward Background.

5. Center Tail on Fuselage and sew. If necessary, straighten sides. Press seam toward Tail.

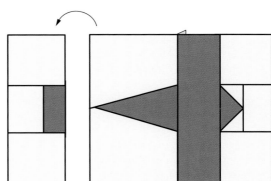

6. Measure. Sliver trim equally on sides if larger.

12" Finished Block	6" Finished Block
7½" x 12½"	4⅛" x 6½"

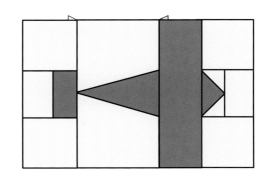

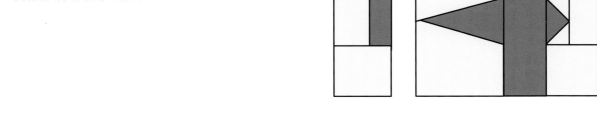

Finishing Block

1. Sew dark Corners to Background sides.

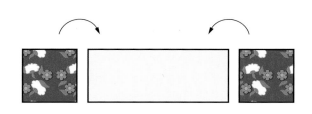

12" Finished Block	6" Finished Block
3" squares	1¾" squares
3" x 7½"	1¾" x 4⅛"

2. **Press one seam toward dark, and one seam toward Background.**

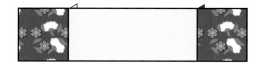

3. Place right sides together to Airplane, lock seams, and sew.

4. Set seams, open, and press toward Background sides.

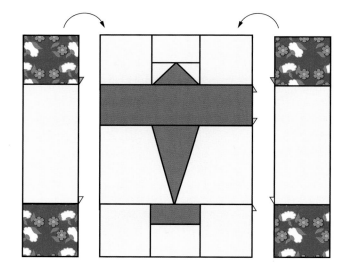

5. Measure and record in box.

12" Finished Block	6" Finished Block
12½" is ideal size	*6½" is ideal size*

It is important that all blocks be one consistent size.

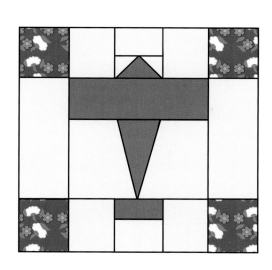

Both of these Airplane quilts are antiques. The one on the left was hand quilted recently. Note the small airplanes quilted on the blue squares. It was made from a commercial pattern in the 1940's.

The quilt on the right is an appliqued quilt with no batting and backing, and is probably is an original design.

68" x 85"

73" x 88"

Optional: Add yellow Stars and Propeller made on paper backed fusible web to Airplane.

For 6" Block

For 12" Block

Trace Stars and/or Propeller on paper side of paper backed fusible web. Center patterns with rough fusible side against wrong side of fabric. Place and hold heated iron on paper side of fusible web for 2 seconds. Cut out patterns on lines, and peel off paper backing. Press in place for 8-10 seconds. Finish outside raw edges with straight stitch.

Fly Boy Quilt

Make six 12" Propeller blocks and six
12" Airplane blocks. Set blocks together
with Lattice and Cornerstones following directions beginning on page 220.
(Straight Set Blocks) Insert rickrack
between First and Second Border.

57" x 72"
Pieced by Teresa Varnes
Quilted by Carol Selepec

Six 12" Propeller Blocks and Six 12" Airplane Blocks

Background	**3½ yds**
Six Airplane Blocks	(2) 4⅛" strips cut into
	(12) 4⅛" x 5¼"
	(5) 3" strips cut into
	(12) 3" x 7½"
	(6) 2" x 3"
	(24) 2¾" x 3"
	(1) 1¾" strip cut into
	(12) 1¾" squares
	(6) 1¾" x 3"
Six Propeller Blocks	(3) 2⅞" strips cut into
	(6) 2⅞" squares
	(6) 2⅞" x 13"
Lattice	(11) 2½" strips cut into
	(31) 2½" x 12½"
First Border	(6) 2½" strips
Second Border	(7) 6" strips
Light Blue Print	**⅝ yd**
Six Propeller Blocks	(3) 6" strips cut into
	(6) 6" x 12"
Medium Red Polka Dot	**⅝ yd**
Six Propeller Blocks	(3) 6" strips cut into
	(6) 6" x 12"
Medium Blue	**⅜ yd**
Airplane	(1) 3½" strip cut into
	(6) 3½" x 6"
	(2) 2¾" strips cut into
	(6) 2¾" x 7½"
	(1) 1¾" strip cut into
	(6) 1¾" x 3"
	(1) 1½" strip cut into
	(6) 1½" x 3"
Dark	**1⅓ yds**
Six Airplane Blocks	(3) 3" strips cut into
	(24) 3" squares
Six Propeller Blocks	(2) 2⅞" strips cut into
	(6) 2⅞" x 13"
Cornerstones	(2) 2½" strips cut into
	(20) 2½" squares
Binding	(7) 3" strips
Rickrack	**6½ yds**
Backing	3¾ yds
Batting	66" x 80"

Hope of Hartford

Supporting American troops abroad was the primary patriotic focus during World War 11. Boy Scouts and Girls Scouts participated in the war effort in many ways. Boy Scouts took part in scrap drives, collecting tin, aluminum, rags and tires for recycling into war materials. Girl Scouts knitted socks for soldiers. Children also dug in and assisted their parents with their Victory Gardens, especially when most food supplies were being sent to soldiers overseas.

The whole country was suffering from the throes of the Great depression but in March, 1936, the folks in Hartford, Connecticut had more problems to contend with. The state was blanketed with six to eight inches of snow when it began to rain. The rain continued for nine days, pouring some fourteen inches on already saturated and frozen ground. The city was paralyzed by torrents of raging waters and ice flows. Bridges, roads, highways, and railways were destroyed as the raging waters tore through the city, devastating everything in its path. Fourteen thousand people were left homeless, several were dead or missing, and epidemic disease threatened the population.

By December 8, 1941, when America declared war on Japan, Connecticut acted as the source of critical war supplies. A good portion of Connecticut's entire industrial capacity was harnessed for military purposes. Whether making products or conserving them for strategic uses, holding rallies for War Bond sales, or organizing air patrols to fortify and guard the coast against enemy attack, Connecticut had again converted itself into an arsenal.

The Hope of Hartford is a tribute to those tenacious and patriotic people who, through Depression and natural disaster, rose to the call to do their part for America's victories in World War II.

Skill Level ★

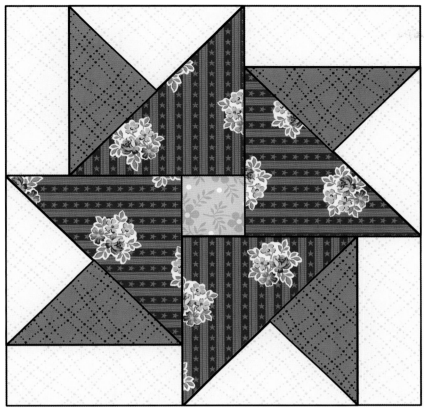

Farm Journal, February – 1945

Supplies

12" Block
6½" Triangle Square Up Ruler
12½" Square Up Ruler
6" x 12" Ruler

6" Block
6½" Triangle Square Up Ruler
9½" Square Up Ruler
6" x 12" Ruler

	12" Finished Block	6" Finished Block
Background		
Little Star Points	(1) 6½" square	(1) 3¾" square
Star Points	(4) 2½" x 5½"	(4) 1¾" x 2⅞"
Medium		
Center Square	(1) 2½" square	(1) 1¾" square
Dark Medium		
Little Star Points	(1) 6½" square	(1) 3¾" square
Dark		
Large Star Points	(2) 6" squares	(2) 3½" squares

Making Little Points of Star

1. With 6" x 12" Ruler, draw two diagonal lines on wrong side of Background square.

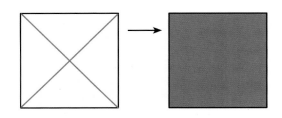

12" Finished Block	6" Finished Block
6½" square	3¾" square

2. Place marked **Background** square right sides together to same size dark medium square and pin.

3. Turn. Sew ¼" from left side of diagonal line and stop at crossing diagonal line.

4. Leave needle in fabric, pivot, and sew on pencil line stopping ¼" past first diagonal line.

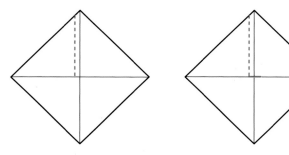

5. Pivot again and stitch ¼" from diagonal line.

6. Repeat on second diagonal line.

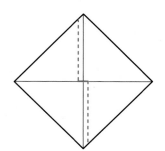 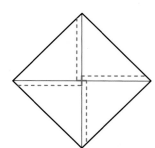

7. Press square.

8. Cut square apart on both **drawn** diagonal lines into four triangles.

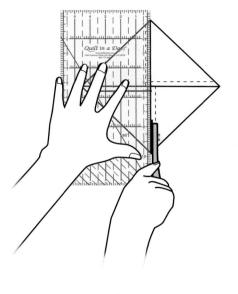

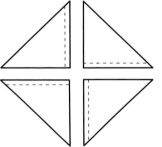

9. Stack triangles with medium on top.

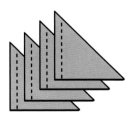

10. Open and press seams to medium.

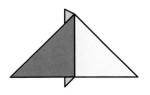

Making Star Points

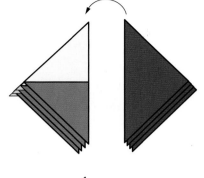

1. Cut two Large Star Points squares in half on one diagonal.

12" Finished Block	6" Finished Block
6" squares	3½" squares

2. Lay out two stacks of triangles.

3. Flip Star Points triangle on right onto Background/ medium triangle on left. **They will not match up exactly.** Line up center point and long edge of both triangles as close as possible.

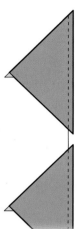

4. Assembly-line sew triangles. Cut apart.

5. Square with 6½" Triangle Square Up Ruler.

12" Finished Block	6" Finished Block
5½" red dotted line	2⅞" green solid line

12" Block
Place **red dashed 5½" line on ruler** slightly above horizontal stitching line to compensate for fold. Place ruler's vertical line on vertical stitching line. Trim two sides.

6" Block
Place **green solid 2⅞" lines on outside edges** of ruler slightly above horizontal stitching line to compensate for fold. Place ruler's vertical line on vertical stitching line. Trim two sides.

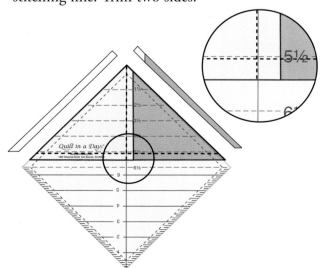

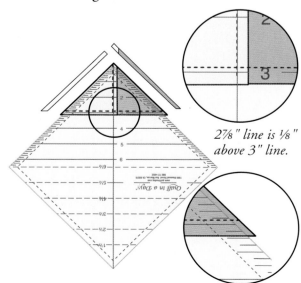

2⅞" line is ⅛" above 3" line.

6. Set seam with dark on top, open, and press toward dark.

7. Trim tips.

8. Place four Star Points with four Background strips. Flip Star Point right sides together to Background strip.

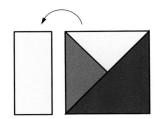

12" Finished Block	6" Finished Block
2½" x 5½"	1¾" x 2⅞"

9. Assembly-line sew.

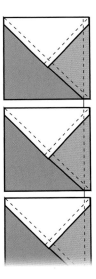

10. Set seam with Background on top. Open, and press toward Background.

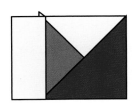

Sewing Block Together

1. Lay out block. Numbers represent the order to sew blocks together.

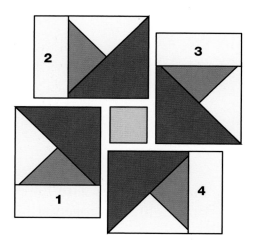

2. Flip Center square right sides together to first Star Point.

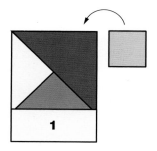

12" Finished Block	6" Finished Block
2½" center square	1¾" center square

3. Sew half way down Center and stop. Set seam with Center on top. Open, and press seam toward Center.

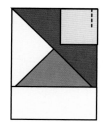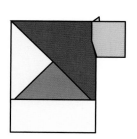

4. Place with second Star Point. Line up straight edges and sew.

5. Press seam toward Center.

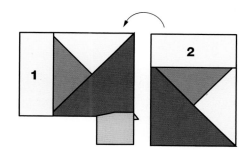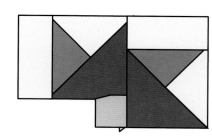

6. Place third Star Point. Flip right sides together and sew from straight edges. Press seam toward Center.

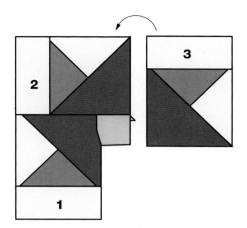

7. Pull first Star Point out of way, and push seam toward Center. Sew fourth Star Point.

8. Complete sewing seam on first Star Point to fourth Star Point. Push seam toward Center.

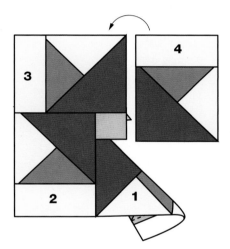

9. Press seams around Center.

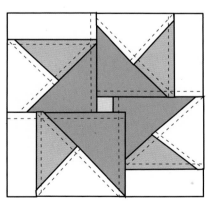

10. Measure and record in box.

12" Finished Block	6" Finished Block
12½" is ideal size	*6½" is ideal size*

It is important that all blocks be one consistent size.

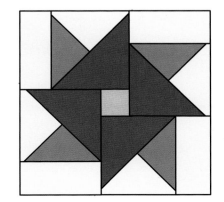

Hope of Hartford Quilt

66" x 82"
Pieced by Eleanor Burns
Quilted by Janna Mitchell

Yardage for Twelve 12" Finished Blocks, Straight Setting and Ribbon Border

Twelve 12" Blocks

**Ribbon Border
4" Finished Size**

(56) Little and Large Points

(4) Corners

Background		**4¼ yds**
Blocks	Little Star Points	(2) 6½" strips cut into (12) 6½" squares
	Star Point Rectangles	(3) 5½" strips cut into (48) 5½" x 2½"
Setting	Lattice	(11) 2½" strips cut into (31) 2½" x size of block
	First Border for Sides	(3) 2⅝" strips
	First Border for Top/Bottom	(3) 3⅝" strips
	Second Border	(8) 6" strips
Ribbon Border	Little Points	(2) 5½" strips cut into (14) 5½" squares
	Corners	(2) 5" squares
Red		**¾ yd**
Blocks	Center Squares	(1) 2½" strip cut into (12) 2½" squares
Setting	Cornerstones	(2) 2½" strips cut into (20) 2½" squares
Ribbon Border	Little Points	(2) 5½" strips cut into (14) 5½" squares
	Corners	(2) 5" squares
Medium Blue		**½ yd**
Blocks	Little Star Points	(2) 6½" strips cut into (12) 6½" squares
Dark Blue		**2 yds**
Blocks	Large Star Points	(4) 6" strips cut into (24) 6" squares
Ribbon Border	Large Star Points	(4) 5" strips cut into (28) 5" squares
	Binding	(7) 3" strips
	Backing	5 yds
	Batting	76" x 90"

1. As you cut, carefully separate pieces into stacks for blocks, Ribbon Border, and Setting.

2. Make twelve Hope of Hartford 12" blocks following directions beginning on page 163.

3. Sew blocks together in Straight Setting with Ribbon Border following directions beginning on page 220.

Liberty Star

September 2, 1945 marked the end of World War II and people around the world rejoiced. After 6 long years the War was over and soldiers would be coming home, prisoners released, and civilians liberated.

Recognizing the Liberty Star block is an especially appropriate way of celebrating the end of an era, World War II. It is a strong and proud symbol of patriotic pride and freedom.

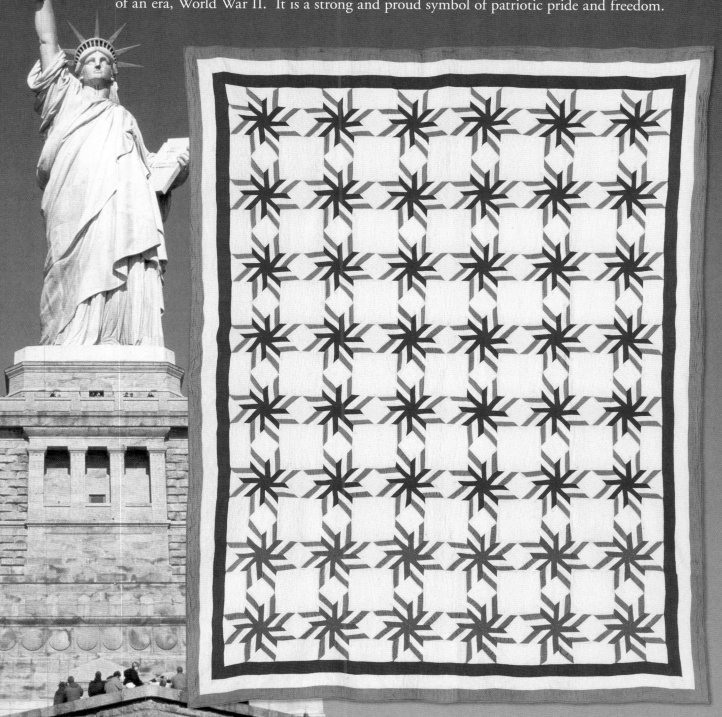

Skill Level ★★★

Supplies

12" Block
6" x 12" Ruler
6" x 24" Ruler
6" Square Up Ruler
12½" Square Ruler
Sharp marking pencil

6" Block
6" x 12" Ruler
6" Square Up Ruler
6½" Triangle Square Up Ruler
Sharp marking pencil

	12" Finished Block	6" Finished Block
Background		
Stripe	(1) 1⅜" x 40" strip or (2) 1⅜" x 21"	(2) 1" x 13"
Light		
Corners	(1) 4⅜" x 18" cut into (4) 4⅜" squares	(1) 2½" x 11" cut into (4) 2½" squares
Side Triangles	(1) 6¾" square	(1) 4" square
Medium		
Stripe	(1) 1⅜" x 40" strip or (2) 1⅜" x 21"	(2) 1" x 13"
Dark		
Stripe	(1) 1⅜" x 40" strip or (2) 1⅜" x 21"	(2) 1" x 13"

Making Eight Diamonds

1. Lay out three strips lengthwise with Background in the middle.

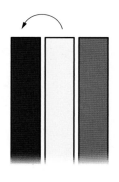

12" Finished Block	6" Finished Block
1⅜" strips	1" strips

2. Sew Background to dark. **Do not use a scant ¼" seam.**

3. Set seam with dark on top, open, and press to dark.

4. Sew medium to Background.

5. Set seam with medium on top, open, and press toward medium.

6. Measure sewn together strip set. **It must be this measurement to create a diamond with equal sides.** Sliver trim or resew if necessary.

12" Finished Block	6" Finished Block
3" strip	1¾" strip

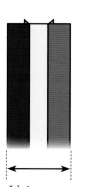

It's important to measure at this step.

7. With 6" x 12" Ruler, line up ruler's 45° line on top edge of strip. Trim selvages. Discard.

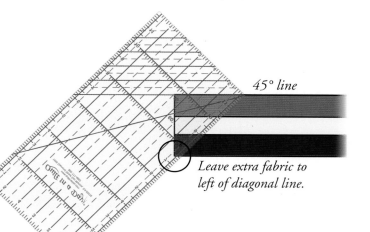

45° line

Leave extra fabric to left of diagonal line.

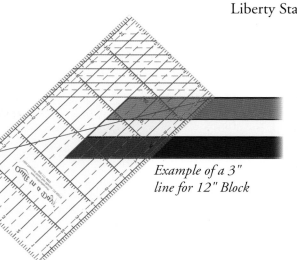

8. Slide 45° line to right across top edge of strip. Line up diagonal cut with designated line. Cut.

12" Finished Block	6" Finished Block
3" line	1¾" line

Example of a 3" line for 12" Block

9. Continue to cut a total of eight diamonds.

10. Divide the eight diamonds into two equal stacks.

11. Flip first diamond on right onto first diamond on left.

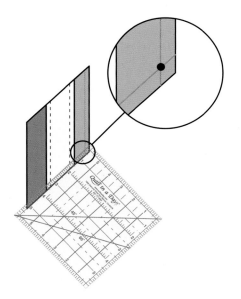

12. With a marking pencil and a 6" Ruler, place a dot ¼" in on end of each pair of diamonds. Pin through dot.

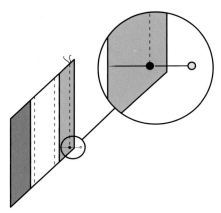

13. Sew diamonds together from center point to dot ¼" from edge. Do not backstitch. Sew all diamonds together.

14. Set seam with medium across top. Open, and gently press seam toward medium.

15. Check from wrong side.

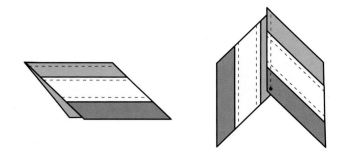

16. Place 6" Ruler's diagonal line on seam. Sliver trim corners of Diamonds.

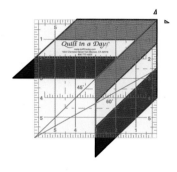

 ## Sewing Corners to Diamonds

1. Turn four Corner squares wrong side up.

12" Finished Block	6" Finished Block
4⅜" squares	2½" squares

2. With a sharp marking pencil, place a small dot ¼" in on one corner of each square.

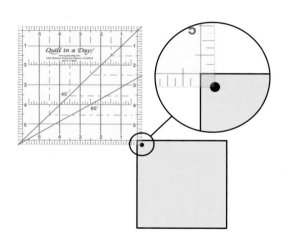

3. Place Diamonds and Corners right side up. Corners are inset in Diamonds by matching dots on square and end of seam on Diamond.

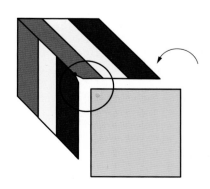

4. Open Diamond to expose unsewn ¼" seam. Flip Corner right sides together to Diamond.

5. Push pin through marked dot on Corner into dot on Diamond.

6. Sew from pin to end of square. Remove pin.

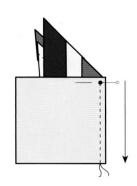

7. Swing Corner to second side of Diamond and line up raw edges. Sew from dot to edge from Diamond side.

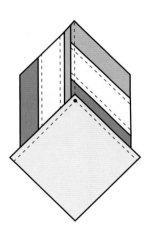

8. Place on pressing mat wrong side up.

9. Press seams away from Corner square.

10. Repeat on remaining Corners.

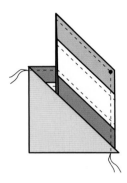

11. Line up ruler with straight sides, and trim tips.

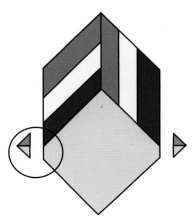

Sewing Star Together

1. Lay out Star.

2. Flip right half of Star onto left half of Star.

3. Lock center seams. Mark dots ¼" in on top and bottom, and pin.

4. Sew together with ¼" seam, beginning and ending on dot ¼" in from edge. Do not clip connecting thread.

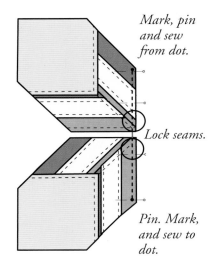

Mark, pin and sew from dot.

Lock seams.

Pin. Mark, and sew to dot.

5. Open and turn. Mark dots ¼" in, and pin. Sew remaining row.

6. At connecting thread, push top seam up, and underneath seam down.

7. Clip connecting thread, and remove straight stitches on both sides. Red thread on left represents stitches to remove.

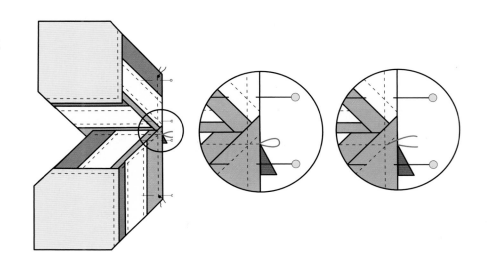

8. Lay block flat wrong side up.

9. Open center and press flat, swirling seams around center.

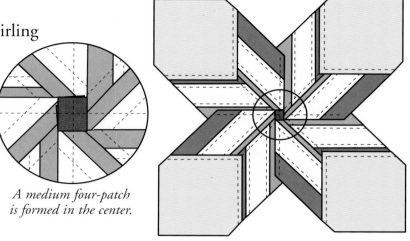

A medium four-patch is formed in the center.

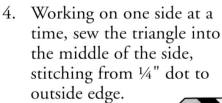 Sewing Side Triangles to Star

1. Turn square for Side Triangles wrong side up.

12" Finished Block	6" Finished Block
6¾" square	4" square

2. Cut square into fourths on diagonals.

3. With a marking pencil, place dot in corner of triangle ¼" in from outside edge.

4. Working on one side at a time, sew the triangle into the middle of the side, stitching from ¼" dot to outside edge.

5. Flip and sew the other side of triangle into other side.

6. Press seams toward triangle.

7. Repeat with remaining Side Triangles.

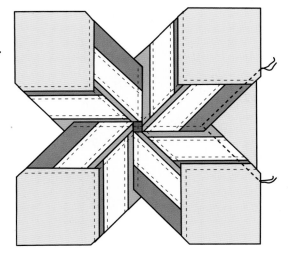

8. Square block, allowing **at least a ¼" seam** from points of Star.

12" Finished Block	6" Finished Block
Square to 12½" with 12½" Square Ruler	Square to 6½" with 6½" Triangle Square Up Ruler

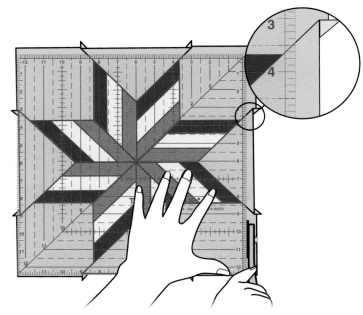

Place 45° line on diagonal seam across center.

9. Measure and record in box.

12" Finished Block	6" Finished Block
12½" is ideal size	*6½" is ideal size*

It is important that all blocks be one consistent size.

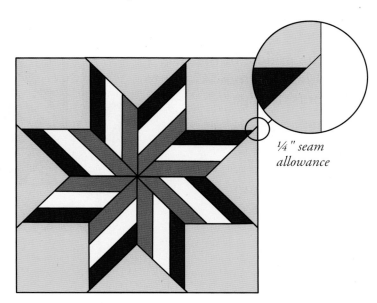

¼" seam allowance

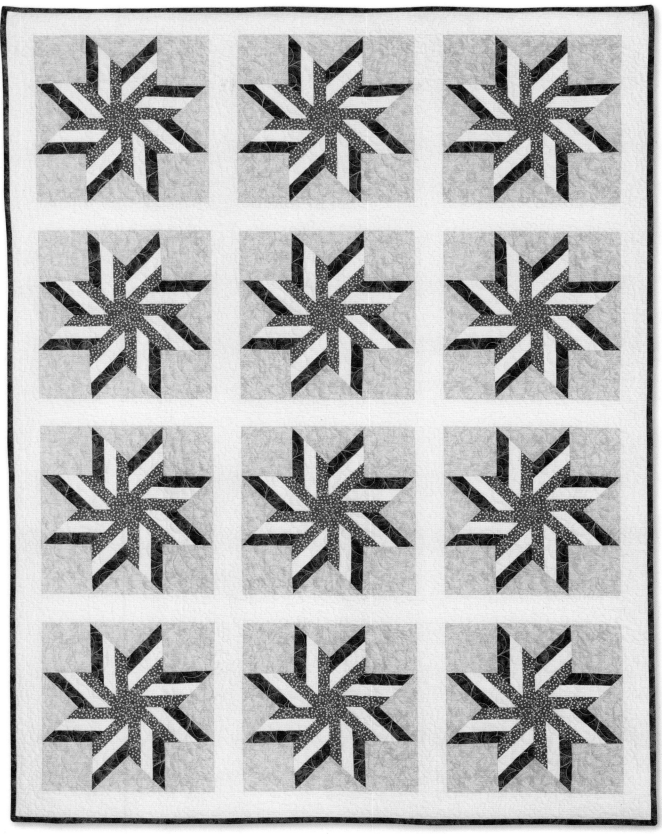

Teresa made this quilt while studying for her U.S. citizenship. She loves the block, and the name of it. She asked everyone at Quilt in a Day in her cute Spanish accent, "Who said, 'Give me liberty or give me death.'?" She had the quilt completed by the time she passed the test.

43" x 56"
Pieced by Teresa Varnes
Quilted by Carol Selepec

Victory Block

Victory in Europe was declared on Tuesday, May 8, 1945, marking the end of six years of pain, courage, and endurance across the world. Some celebrated, while others spent the day in quiet reflection while mourning the loss of FDR on April 12. Nothing would be the same again! Hitler committed suicide on April 30, so the surrender was authorized by his replacement.

On August 6, the United States dropped an atomic bomb on Hiroshima, and three days later on Nagasaki. Japan surrendered on August 14, 1945.

Alfred Eisenstaedt took this famous photograph in Times Square on August 14. The kissing couple summed up the national mood with the returning soldier, the woman who welcomed him back, and New York, the crossroads that symbolized home. Wildly jubilant celebrators tooted horns, staged parades, and dropped paper from skyscrapers.

Within one week, most women had been fired from their job. It ended a time in America when women were told that they could do anything.

Skill Level ★★★

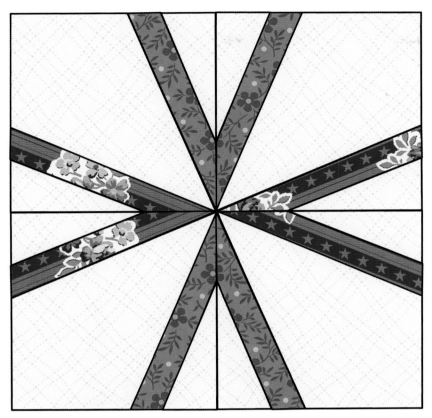

V Block, Ladies Art Company, #483
Victory Quilt, Georgette Pattern Company – 1945
Churchill Block, Evelyn Brown

Supplies

12" Block
6½" Fussy Cut Ruler
12½" Square Up Ruler
6" x 24" Ruler

6" Block
3½" Fussy Cut Ruler
9½" Square Up Ruler
6" x 24" Ruler

	12" Finished Block	6" Finished Block
Background		
Background	(1) 9¾" x 20"	(1) 5½" x 11"
Edge Triangles	(4) 3" x 6"	(4) 2¼" x 4¼"
Medium		
V Shape	(4) 1½" x 11"	(4) 1" x 6"
Dark		
V Shape	(4) 1½" x 11"	(4) 1" x 6"

Making Four V Blocks

Two V blocks are made mirror image.

1. Glue photocopy of V template on template plastic, and cut out.

2. Trace four V's on Background, and cut out.

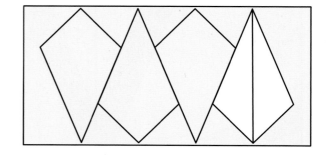

12" Finished Block	6" Finished Block
9¾" x 20"	5½" x 11"

3. Stack two medium strips with two Background shapes.

4. Stack two dark strips with two Background shapes.

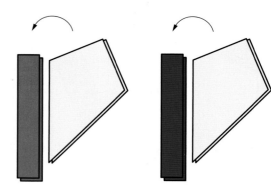

12" Finished Block	6" Finished Block
1½" x 11"	1" x 6"

5. Flip Background right sides together to strip. Line up ¼" from top edge.

6. Assembly-line sew.

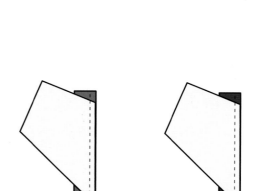

Line up ¼" from top edge.

7. From wrong side, press seams open with fingernails. Carefully press with iron.

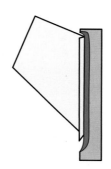

8. Line up diagonal line on Fussy Cut Ruler with left strip and right side of ruler with Background. Trim one end only.

12" Finished Block	6" Finished Block
6½" Fussy Cut Ruler	3½" Fussy Cut Ruler

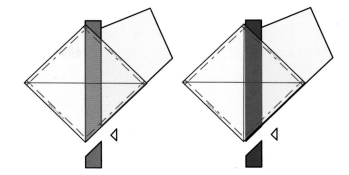

9. Turn. Place opposite color strips on left side of Background.

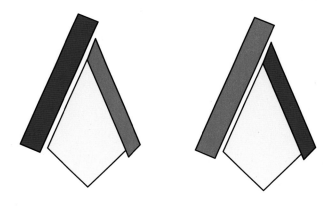

10. Flip right sides together, matching ¼" from bottom end. Assembly-line sew.

11. From wrong side, press seams open.

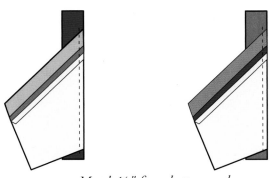

Match ¼" from bottom end.

12. Line up diagonal line on Fussy Cut Ruler with side of left strip and straight edge of ruler with right strip. Trim.

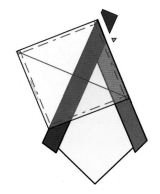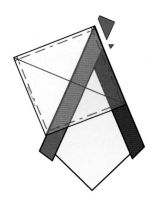

13. Turn patch. Match tip of ruler with tip of Background and sides. Line up diagonal line on ruler with point on strips. Trim ends.

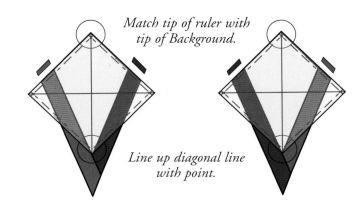

Match tip of ruler with tip of Background.

Line up diagonal line with point.

◈ Adding Edge Triangles

1. Place two pairs of Background rectangles right sides together.

12" Finished Block	6" Finished Block
3" x 6"	2¼" x 4¼"

2. Cut on one diagonal. Turn right side up.

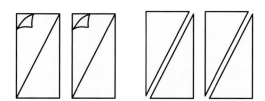

3. Place bias edge of Triangles with V Block right side up. **Outside Triangle edges are on the straight of grain.**

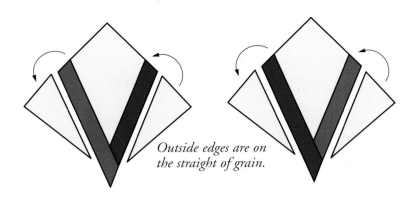

Outside edges are on the straight of grain.

4. Flip right sides together. Allow **½"** to hang over on top edge. Sew.

Allow ½" to hang over.

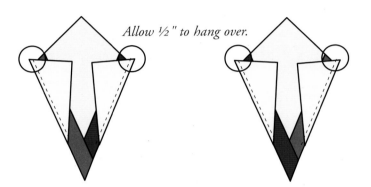

5. From wrong side, press seams in different directions so seams lock in finished block.

First Block
Press seam toward dark and away from medium.

Second Block
Press seam toward medium, and away from dark.

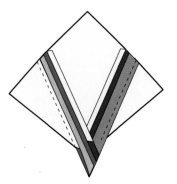

Squaring Up Block

1. Place block right side up.

2. Place Fussy Cut Ruler on block.

12" Finished Block	6" Finished Block
6½" Fussy Cut Ruler	3½" Fussy Cut Ruler

3. Carefully place ¼" lines on top seam lines. Place ruler's diagonal line into bottom point on Background triangle.

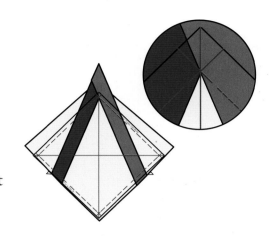
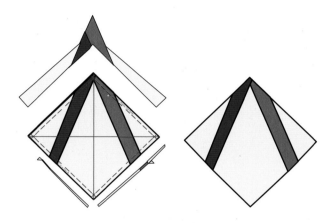

4. Trim around ruler on four sides.

Sewing Block Together

1. Lay out block.

2. Flip right vertical row to left vertical row, right sides together.

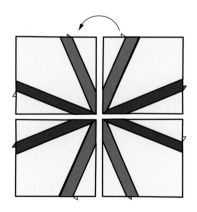

3. Assembly-line sew, locking circled seams. Do not clip connecting threads.

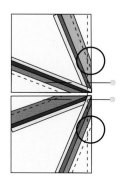

4. Turn block. Lock circled seams. Press top seam up, and underneath seam down. Sew.

5. Check from right side. The center seam is very thick, and sometimes shifts. If middle doesn't match from right side, check seam width from wrong side. It may be less than ¼". If so, sew again with deeper seam.

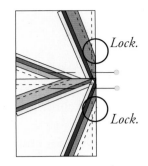

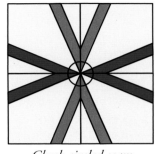

Check circled seam.

6. Turn to wrong side. Clip connecting thread in center and remove approximately three straight stitches on both sides. See red thread.

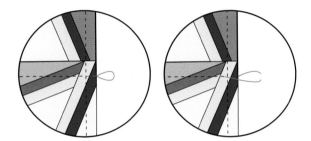

7. Place on pressing mat wrong side up. Push top vertical seam to right, and bottom vertical seam to left. Center will pop open and make a little pinwheel.

8. Press center flat with your finger. Press seams so they swirl around center.

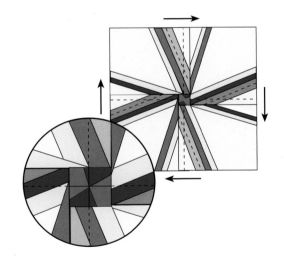

9. Measure and record in box.

12" Finished Block	6" Finished Block
12½" is ideal size	*6½" is ideal size*

It is important that all blocks be one consistent size.

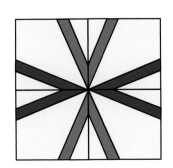

Bride's Bouquet

During World War II, many women arranged wartime weddings within a few days to accommodate the future husband coming home on a short leave before being sent overseas. There was no time to get a special dress, nor could they afford the rationed clothing coupons needed for a wedding dress. Besides, they needed to buy clothing that would be useful after the wedding event. Typically, the bride and her maid of honor wore utility suits in grayish blues, beiges or other neutral tones. She possibly carried a bouquet of chrysanthemums, a flower typically used in bridal bouquets.

During and after the war, it was quite usual for men serving in the navy, air or armed forces, to marry in their uniform or dress uniform. War brides accepted this. No matter what they wore, they were happy!

Weddings took place with family members often donating small amounts of rationed items as sugar, flour, and eggs so that the bride could bake a wedding cake. Gardens were raided for flowers, and relatives would beautify the private home for the special occasion.

Ida Mary Decola and Ken Bouchard,
June 9, 1946
Chicago, Illinois

Skill Level ★★★

Bride's Bouquet – Rural New Yorker

Supplies

12" Block
Template Plastic
6" x 12" Ruler
6½" Triangle Square Up Ruler
6" Square Up Ruler
12½" Square Up Ruler

6" Block
Template Plastic
6" x 12" Ruler
6½" Triangle Square Up Ruler
6" Square Up Ruler

	12" Finished Block	6" Finished Block
Background		
Five Squares	(1) 2¾" x 11"	(1) 1¾" x 8"
	(1) 2¾" x 22"	(1) 1¾" x 14"
Sides of Handle	(2) 3¼" x 10¾"	(2) 2" x 6⅛"
Light		
Five Squares	(1) 2" x 11"	(1) 1¼" x 8"
Medium		
Handle	(2) 3" x 10½"	(2) 1¾" x 6⅛"
Three Different Mediums		
Diamonds	(1) 3" x 8" of each	(1) 1¾" x 4½" of each
Three Different Darks		
Diamonds	(1) 3" x 8" of each	(1) 1¾" x 4½" of each

191

Sewing Background to Squares

1. Sew strip for Squares to Background strip.

12" Finished Block	6" Finished Block
2" x 11" Squares	1¼" x 8" Squares
2¾" x 11" Background	1¾" x 8" Background

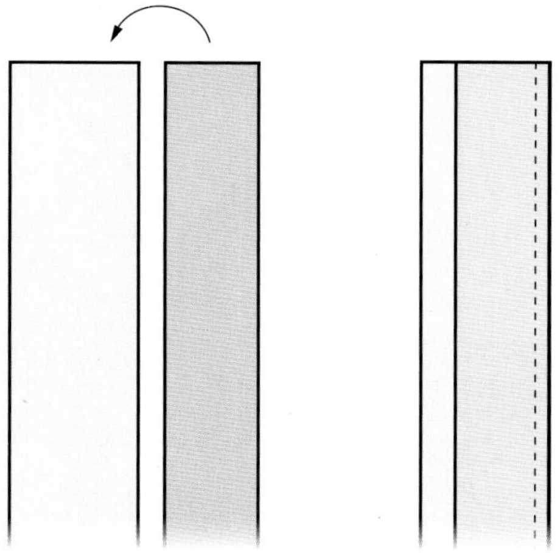

2. Set seam with strip for Squares on top. Open and press toward strip for Squares.

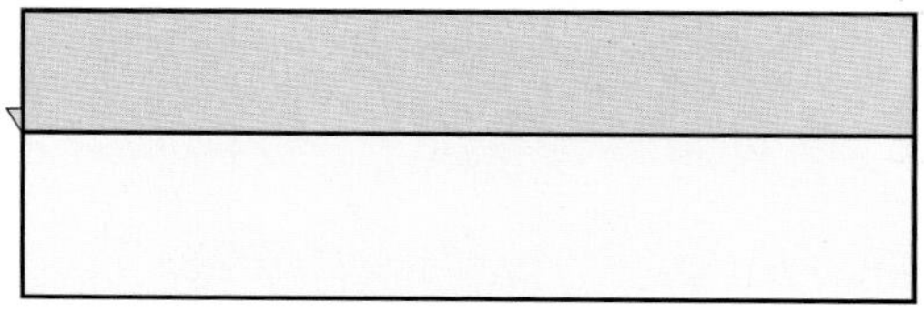

3. Straighten left end. Cut into five pieces.

12" Finished Block	6" Finished Block
2" pieces	1¼" pieces

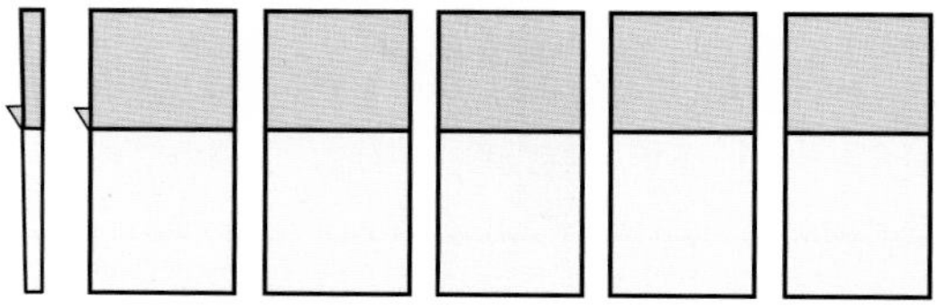

4. Place pieces with wider Background strip. Flip right sides together, and assembly-line sew.

12" Finished Block	6" Finished Block
2¾" x 22"	1¾" x 14"

5. Set seam with Background on top, open, and press toward Background.

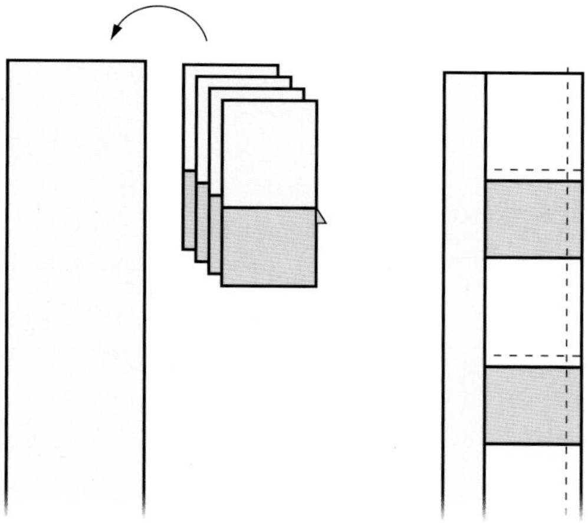

6. Cut apart between patches with 6" Square Up Ruler. Check measurement.

12" Finished Block	6" Finished Block
4¼" squares	2½" squares

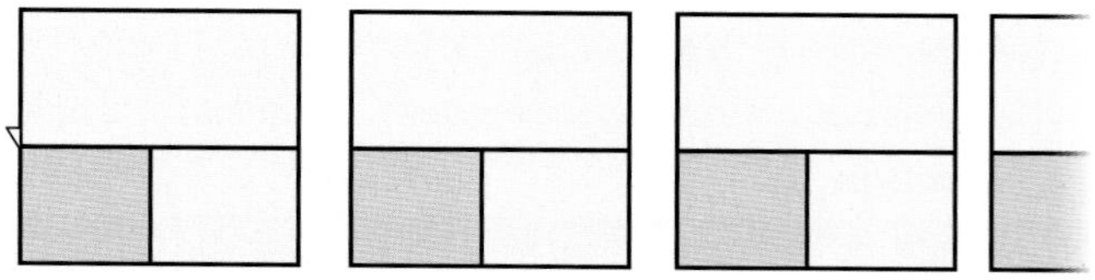

7. Set aside.

Cutting Three Pairs of Diamonds

1. Divide six different Diamond rectangles into three pairs.

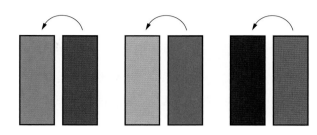

12" Finished Block	6" Finished Block
3" x 8"	1¾" x 4½"

2. Assembly-line sew. Clip apart.

3. Make photocopy of template. Glue to template plastic and cut out.

4. Place diamond template on pair. Draw diagonal lines. Mark three pairs.

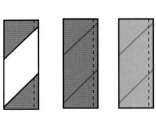

5. Cut on diagonal lines. Discard ends.

discard

discard

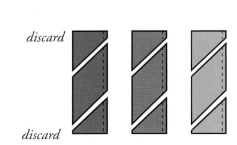

Sewing Pieces Together

This next step is called "Y seaming". It is very similar to inserting Background squares and triangles into Points on Liberty Star, pages 176-180.

1. Turn **three Square patches** wrong side up. Place light dot ¼" from corner on light Square.

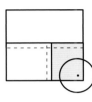

2. Open pair of Diamonds.

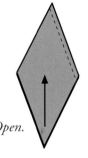

Open.

3. Match tips. Gently pull out ¼" of stitches as you open. Lightly place dot ¼" from edge.

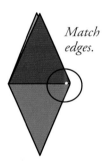

Match edges.

4. Push pin through dot on Square through dot on Diamond.

5. Pin opposite end with ¼" tip hanging out. Sew three sets of Diamonds with Squares.

6. Line up Square with Diamond. Sew from outside edge toward middle, stopping at dot.

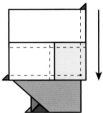

When sewing a seam, be careful to keep all other pieces out of way.

7. Press into Corner from right side.

8. From wrong side, **press Diamond seam to left.**

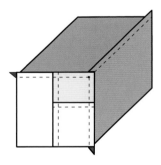

9. Place 6" Square Up Ruler on patch, and trim tips.

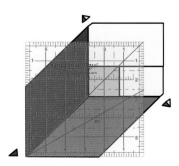

Cutting Pieces for Handle

1. Place Background rectangles for Sides of Handle **right sides together**, and place on cutting mat.

12" Finished Block	6" Finished Block
3¼" x 10¾"	2" x 6⅛"

2. Put diagonal line on 6" x 12" Ruler across top edge. Line up edge of ruler on left corner of rectangles.

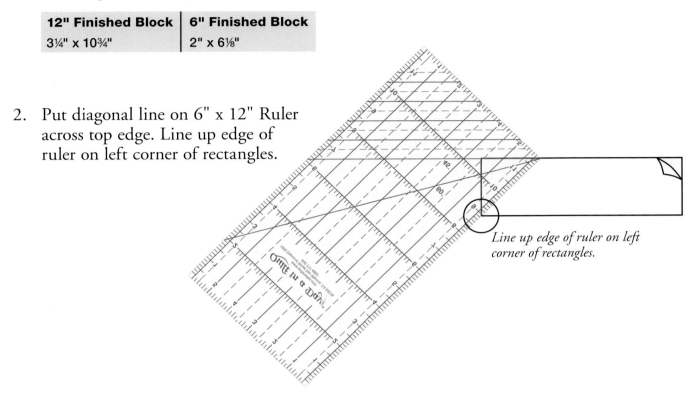

Line up edge of ruler on left corner of rectangles.

3. Cut off 45° angle at left edge. Discard corner.

discard

4. Cut from top edge to bottom right edge with 6" x 12" Ruler. Discard corner.

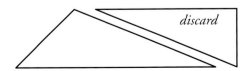

discard

Sewing Handle

1. Place Handle rectangles **right sides together**, and place on cutting mat.

12" Finished Block	6" Finished Block
3" x 10½"	1¾" x 6⅛"

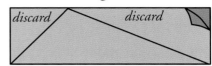

2. Put diagonal line on 6" x 12" Ruler across top edge. Line up edge of ruler on left corner of rectangles.

3. Cut off 45° angle at left edge. Discard corner.

4. Cut from top edge to bottom right edge. Discard corner.

5. **Do not open.** Sew long seam.

6. Turn over and press seam to left.

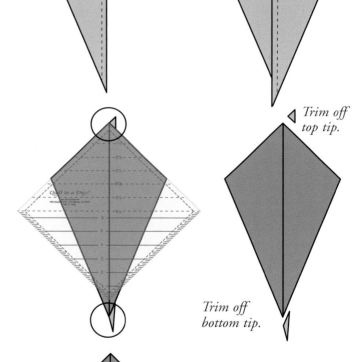

7. Place 6½" Ruler on Handle and trim top at 45° angle, and bottom following lines of fabric.

Trim off top tip.

Trim off bottom tip.

8. Trim ¼" off bottom tip with straight cut.

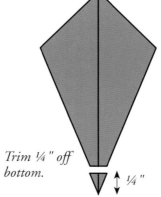

Trim ¼" off bottom.

¼"

Sewing Block Together

1. Lay out pieces. Flip right vertical row to left vertical row.

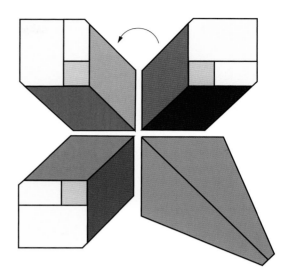

2. Mark ¼" intersecting lines. Pin.

3. Sew, beginning and stopping ¼" from ends. Do not clip connecting threads.

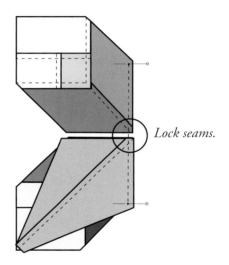

Lock seams.

4. Open pair of Diamonds and turn. Flip right sides together. Pin ¼" from ends.

5. Lock center seam, pushing top seams up, and underneath seams down. Sew.

6. Clip connecting thread. Remove three stitches on front and back. Stitches are indicated by red threads.

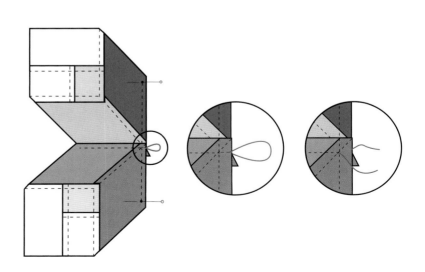

7. Place patch wrong side up. **Press seams clockwise** around center. Press center open into a little four-patch.

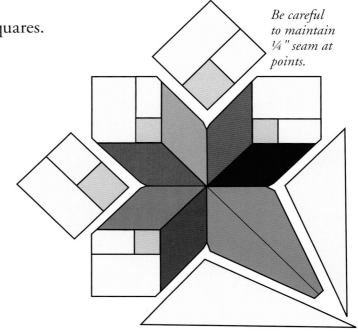

8. Lay out Bouquet with remaining two Squares.

9. Inset pieces with Y seams.

10. Press seams toward Background.

11. Insert right Background Handle.

12. Press seam toward Background. Trim tip following side of Handle.

13. Insert left Background to Handle, and press toward Background.

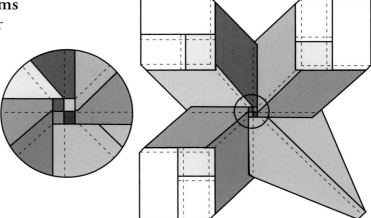

Be careful to maintain ¼" seam at points.

14. Center ruler on patch and trim on all four sides without removing ¼" seam allowance.

12" Finished Block	6" Finished Block
12½" Square Up Ruler	6½" Triangle Square Up Ruler

15. Measure and record.

12" Finished Block	6" Finished Block
12½" is ideal size	*6½" is ideal size*

It is important that all blocks be one consistent size.

85" x 85"
Made by Armelia Gipson Bruce,
Lebanon Boone County, Indiana
1930's

This is a variation of Bride's
Bouquet from Old Chelsea Station by
Wheeler and Brooks. Thirty-six 10" blocks
of Nosegay design have green bases, with mixed
pastel print diamonds representing the flowers, and plain
bright gold quarter circles backing the flowers. The blocks are
set on point with a single orientation, and set alternately with white
squares. The applied binding is plain bright gold, over white back. Entirely
hand pieced and joined, beautifully hand quilted in outline and diamond cross
hatching in the pattern pieces, with feathers filling the block. The white setting squares
have a beautiful lyre with feather marks through the center from long-term storage.

Brave World

After the war, the men returned, having seen the rest of the world. Women had to give up their jobs to the returning men, but they had tasted independence. Anyone who had contact with communism was under suspicion.

Returning GI's created the baby boom, which is still having repercussions on American society today. There was reform over Civil Rights. The GI Bill of Rights entitled returning soldiers to a college education. Three times more college degrees were issued.

In 1947, thirteen commercial television stations became available. The average home was a one level ranch filled with appliances. The front lawn was the symbol of pride in ownership. Times had changed after the war!

Skill Level ★

The Spinner, Nancy Page
Brave World, Farm Journal – 1944

Supplies

12" Block
6" x 12" Ruler
9½" Square Up Ruler
12½" Square Up Ruler
6½" Fussy Cut Ruler

6" Block
6" x 12" Ruler
6½" Triangle Square Up Ruler
3½" Fussy Cut Ruler

	12" Finished Block	6" Finished Block
Background		
Small Triangles	(1) 4½" x 15"	(1) 3" x 9"
Medium		
Squares	(1) 3½" x 15"	(1) 2" x 9"
Dark		
Large Triangles	(2) 6½" x 7½"	(2) 3½" x 4½"

Making Four Corner Patches

This method yields two patches in one operation.

1. Flip medium Square fabric strip right sides together to Background, and sew.

12" Finished Block	6" Finished Block
3½" x 15" Squares	2" x 9" Squares
4½" x 15" Background	3" x 9" Background

2. Set seam with medium Square fabric on top, open, and press toward Square.

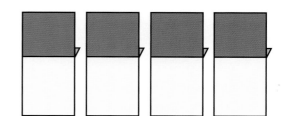

3. Square left end. Cut into four pieces.

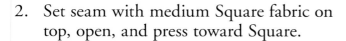

12" Finished Block	6" Finished Block
3½" pieces	2" pieces

4. Lay out pieces. Place two in each stack.

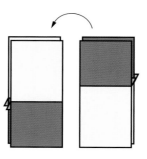

5. Flip right sides together. **Seams do not lock.**

6. Assembly-line sew.

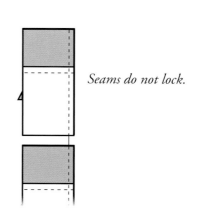

Seams do not lock.

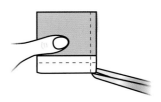

7. Fold in half. Clip seam in the middle to the stitching.

8. Place on pressing mat wrong side up. Press, pushing the clipped seam to the rectangles.

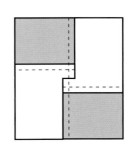

9. Lay diagonal line of ruler on short side of patch.

12" Finished Block	6" Finished Block
Use 9½" Square Up Ruler	Use 6½" Triangle Square Up Ruler

10. Shift the ruler until the ruler's edge is at the point of the Square. **See lower circle.** The point of the ruler should be at the top edge of the patch. **See upper circle.**

11. Draw a pencil line that will be your sewing line. **Do not cut.**

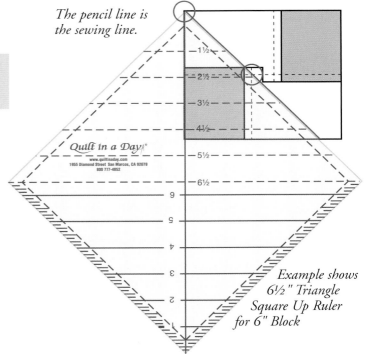

The pencil line is the sewing line.

Quilt in a Day®
www.quiltinaday.com
1955 Diamond Street San Marcos, CA 92078
800 777-4852

Example shows 6½" Triangle Square Up Ruler for 6" Block

12. Turn patch, and draw another sewing line across the point of the other Square. The distance between the parallel lines is **at least ½"**, or two seam allowances.

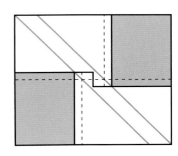

13. Layer patches right sides together with dark rectangles for Large Triangles.

12" Finished Block	6" Finished Block
6½" x 7½"	3½" x 4½"

14. Press and pin.

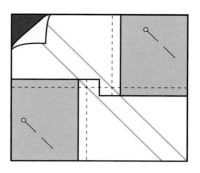

15. Sew on **inside edge** of drawn lines.

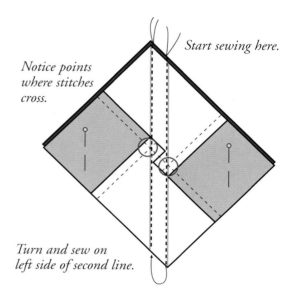

Start sewing here.

Notice points where stitches cross.

Turn and sew on left side of second line.

16. Cut between the lines. Trim seam to ¼".

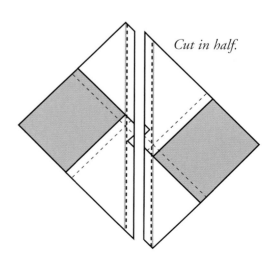

Cut in half.

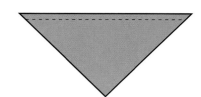

17. Set seams with Triangle on top. Open,
    and press seam to Triangle.

18. Trim tips.

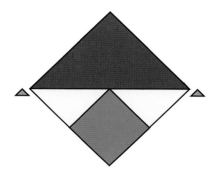

19. Measure patch against Fussy Cut Ruler.
    Sliver trim if necessary.

12" Finished Block	6" Finished Block
6½" Fussy Cut Ruler	3½" Fussy Cut Ruler

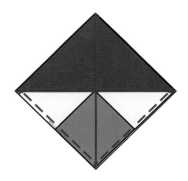

◈ Sewing Block Together

1. Lay out patches.

2. Flip right vertical row right sides together to left vertical row. Lock seams.

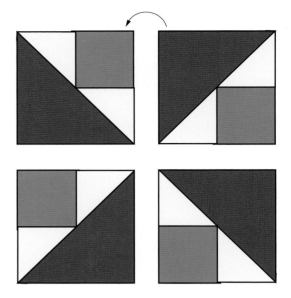

3. Assembly-line sew. Do not clip connecting threads.

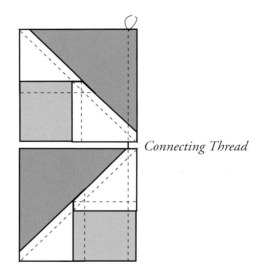

Connecting Thread

4. Turn. Flip row on right to vertical row on left.

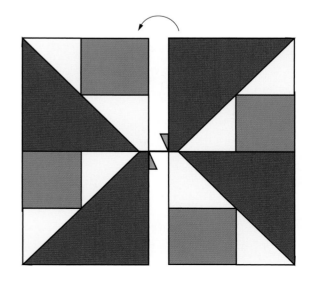

5. Lock seams, pushing top seams up, and underneath seams down. Sew.

6. Clip connecting thread in center and remove approximately three straight stitches on both sides. See red thread.

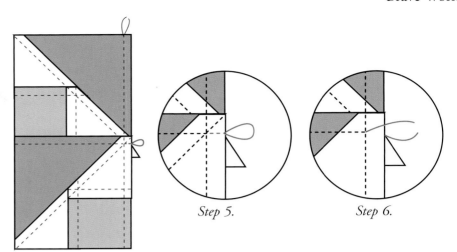

Step 5.   *Step 6.*

7. Place on pressing mat wrong side up. Push top vertical seam to right, and bottom vertical seam to left. Center will pop open and make a little pinwheel.

8. Press center flat with your finger. Press so seams swirl around center.

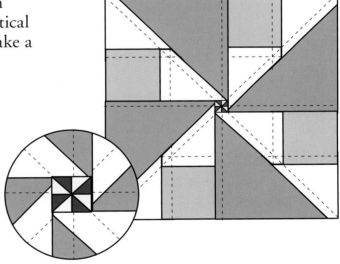

9. Measure and record in box.

12" Finished Block	6" Finished Block
12½ " is ideal size	*6½ " is ideal size*
It is important that all blocks be one consistent size.	

Sewing Quilt Top Together

Sewing On Point Top and Swag Border

Squaring Your Blocks

1. Check that each block is a consistent size approximately 12½" or 6½" square. Your blocks may be consistently 12¼" or 6¼".

   For blocks larger than consistent size, sliver trim without trimming away any part of the ¼" seam allowance. Use a 12½" Square Up Ruler for 12" finished size blocks, and a 6½" Triangle Square Up Ruler for 6" finished size blocks. If necessary, resew a wider seam.

   For blocks smaller than consistent size, check seam widths and pressing. Unsew any wider seams and sew again with narrower seam.

2. Do not be concerned if there is a ¼" variance in block sizes. They can be stretched to size of other blocks.

Cutting Side and Corner Triangles

1. Cut squares for Side Triangles on both diagonals.

12" Finished Block	6" Finished Block
18 Blocks (3) 22½" squares	18 Blocks (3) 12" squares
13 Blocks (2) 22½" squares	13 Blocks (2) 12" squares

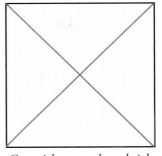
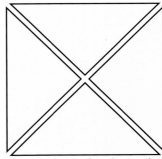

Cut with a metal yardstick or two rulers placed end to end.

2. Cut two squares for Corners on one diagonal.

12" Finished Block	6" Finished Block
14" squares	7½" squares

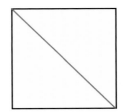
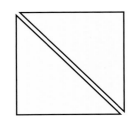

Eighteen Block Setting Only
Sewing Triangle for End of Fourth Diagonal Row

1. Sew one Cornerstone to one Lattice, right sides together.

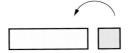

2. Press seam toward Lattice.

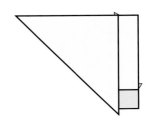

3. Sew Lattice/Cornerstone combination to Side Triangle.

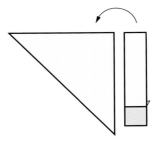

4. Press seam toward Triangle.

Sewing Blocks, Lattice, and Cornerstones Together

1. Lay out your quilt following appropriate illustration. Place blocks in any order you choose so shapes and colors are evenly distributed. Separate into diagonal rows.

2. Sew Lattice and Cornerstone rows together. Press seams toward Lattice.

3. Sew Block and Lattice rows together. Press seams toward Lattice.

Eighteen Blocks

Thirteen Blocks

4. Sew Lattice/Cornerstone rows and Lattice/Block rows together. Press seams toward Lattice.

5. Place Side Triangles on ends of rows.

   Eighteen Block only: Place Lattice/ Cornerstone/Triangle on end of fourth diagonal row.

6. Match 90° angles. Let tip on Triangles hang over.

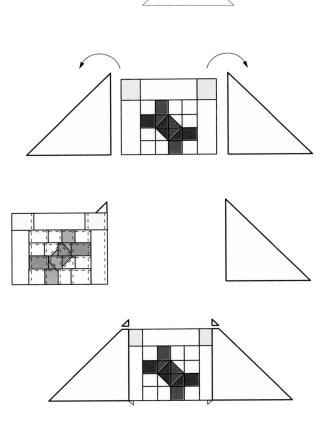

7. Sew with Triangles on bottom so bias doesn't stretch.

8. Press seams toward Lattice.

9. Trim tips from Triangles.

10. Sew rows together, matching Cornerstone and Lattice seams.

11. Press seams away from center.

Adding Corners

1. Fold Corner triangles in half, and crease on fold.

2. Fold corners of top in half, and crease.

3. Match centers of Corners to centers of top. Pin, and sew with triangles on bottom.

4. Press seams toward Corners.

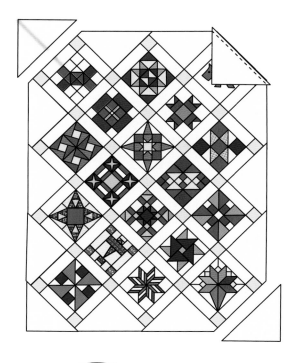

Squaring Outside Edges

1. Press top from wrong side and right side.

2. Lay top flat on cutting area.

3. Square outside edges, leaving ¼" seam allowance.

    • Place Quilt in a Day's 16" Square Up Ruler in upper right corner.

    • Place ruler's ¼" marks on points.

    • Line up diagonal line on ruler with center of block.

    • Trim two sides.

    • Trim remaining corners.

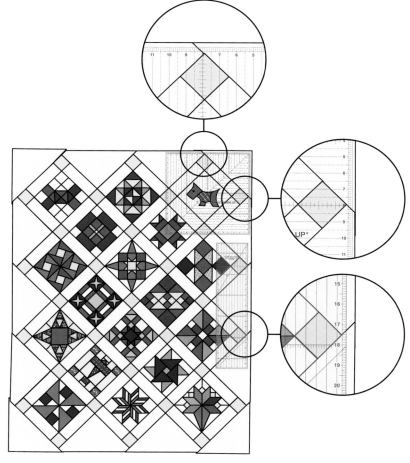

4. Line up 6" x 24" Ruler, and trim between Corners.

Adding Border for Swag

1. Trim selvages from Border strips.

2. If necessary, piece Border strips together.

3. Measure length of both sides, and center of quilt top. Cut two Border strips the average length.

4. Place Borders right sides together to sides of top. Pin layers together in center, on ends, and several places between each. Sew to sides.

5. Set seam with Border on top. Open and press seams toward Border.

6. Measure width. Cut two Border pieces for top and bottom of the average width. Pin and sew. Press seams toward Border.

Adding Plain Border

1. Cut Border strips.

2. Trim away selvages at a right angle.

3. Assembly-line sew all short ends together into long pieces.

4. Cut Border pieces the average length of both sides.

5. Pin and sew to sides. Fold out and press seams toward Border.

6. Measure the width and cut Border pieces for top and bottom. Pin and sew.

7. Press seams toward Border.

67" x 81"
Pieced by Kari Gjerde
Quilted by Amie Potter

Making Swags and Corners

Swags are made with fabric and non-woven fusible interfacing. Outside edges are turned in, and are easy to fuse and sew to quilt top. Stars are made with paper-backed fusible web. Outside edges are raw edges, making points easier to sew.

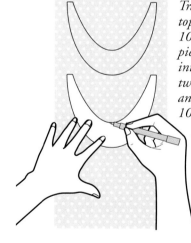

Top Swag

Bottom Swag

Top Corner

Bottom Corner

Make Corners for 12" blocks only.

1. Photocopy top and bottom Swag template for 12" or 6" blocks. **Photocopy top and bottom Corners for 12" blocks only.** Glue to template plastic with glue stick and cut out.

Eighteen 12" Blocks	Thirteen 12" Blocks	Eighteen 6" Blocks	Thirteen 6" Blocks
28 Top Swags	24 Top Swags	18 Top Swags	16 Top Swags
28 Bottom Swags	24 Bottom Swags	18 Bottom Swags	16 Bottom Swags
4 Top Corners	4 Top Corners		
4 Bottom Corners	4 Bottom Corners		

2. Trace Swags on **smooth side** of non-woven fusible interfacing with permanent marking pen. Leave ½" space between pieces.

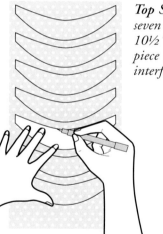

Top Swag Trace seven on each 10½" x 21" piece of fusible interfacing.

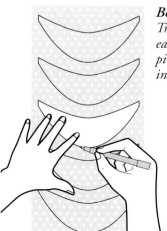

Bottom Swag Trace five on each 10½" x 21" piece of fusible interfacing.

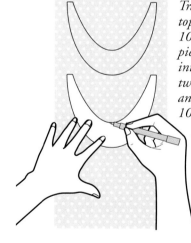

Corners Trace two tops on one 10½" x 21" piece of fusible interfacing, and two bottoms on another piece of 10½" x 21" fusible interfacing.

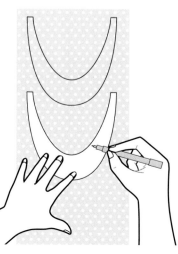

3. Place interfacing marked with Top Swags and Top Corners on medium fabric with **rough fusible side against right side of fabric.** Pin in place.

4. Repeat with Bottom Swags and Bottom Corners on dark fabric.

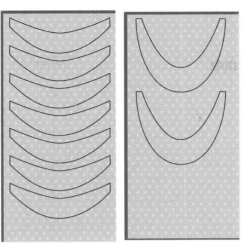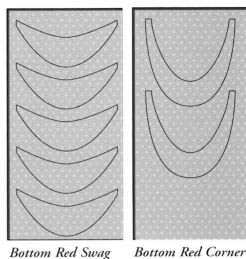

Top Blue Swag   *Top Blue Corner*   *Bottom Red Swag*   *Bottom Red Corner*

Pin Top Swag and Top Corner on medium blue fabric.   *Pin Bottom Swag and Bottom Corner on dark red fabric.*

5. Place open toe applique foot on sewing machine. Lighten pressure on presser foot.

6. Set machine at 18 stitches per inch, or 1.8 stitch length on computerized machines. If available, use needle down position on needle. **Lock seams at beginning and end of stitching.**

Top Blue Swag and Top Blue Corner

1. Sew on lines indicated by dashes.

2. Leave ends open for turning.

Top Blue Swag and Top Blue Corner

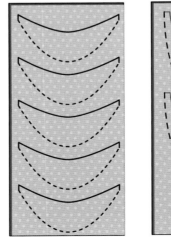

Sew on top and bottom lines. Leaves ends open for turning.

Bottom Red Swag and Bottom Red Corner

1. Solid lines indicate cutting lines.

2. Sew on bottom dashed line only. Leave ends and top line open for turning.

Bottom Red Swag and Bottom Red Corner

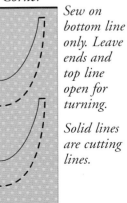

Sew on bottom line only. Leave ends and top line open for turning.

Solid lines are cutting lines.

Trimming and Turning Swags

1. Trim ⅛" away from stitching. Trim ends.

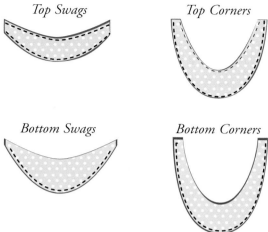

Top Swags   *Top Corners*

Bottom Swags   *Bottom Corners*

2. Turn Bottom Swags and Bottom Corners right side out with fingers.

3. Smooth curves by running ball point bodkin or point turner around inside edge of each piece.

4. With wooden iron or thumb nail, press edge of fabric over interfacing. As an alternative, press with steam iron on applique pressing sheet.

Bottom Swags and Bottom Corners

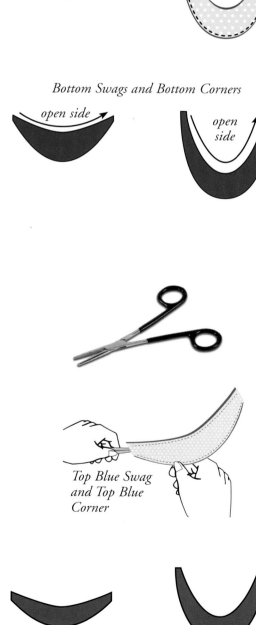

open side   *open side*

5. Use hemostat to turn Top Swags and Top Corners.

6. Insert hemostat in open end, push tip of hemostat to opposite end, and firmly grasp fabric. Pull carefully, turning Swags and Corners right side out.

Top Blue Swag and Top Blue Corner

7. Smooth curves by running ball point bodkin around inside edge of each piece.

8. Press edge of fabric over interfacing.

Overlapping Top and Bottom Swags and Corners

1. Mark centers on ends of Bottom Red Swag and Bottom Corner with chalk or permanent marking pen.

2. Overlap Top Blue Swag on Red Swag, lining up bottom edge of Blue Swag with top of centered mark on Red Swag.

3. Place on applique pressing sheet.

4. Fuse together with steam.

5. Cool and set aside.

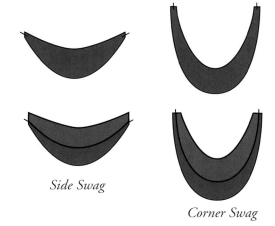

Side Swag

Corner Swag

Making Stars

Stars are made on paper back-fusible web, and fused in place. Outside edges are raw. If you prefer, you can make Stars with fusible interfacing and quick turn. Outside edges are finished the same as the Swags.

1. Make small Star templates for 12" and 6" blocks, and large Star for 6" only.

2. Trace Stars on paper side of paper backed fusible web.

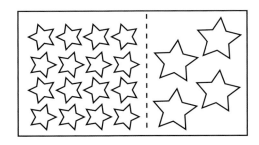

Eighteen 12" Block Quilt	32 Small Stars
Thirteen 12" Block Quilt	28 Small Stars
Eighteen 6" Block Quilt	14 Small Stars
	4 Large Stars
Thirteen 6" Block Quilt	12 Small Stars
	4 Large Stars

3. Place Star fabric wrong side up on pressing mat. **Center Stars with rough fusible side of paper against wrong side of fabric. Paper should be slightly smaller than fabric.**

4. Pre-heat dry iron to silk setting. Do not use steam.

5. Place and hold heated iron on paper side of fusible web for **2 seconds**.

6. Cut out Stars on lines, and peel off paper backing.

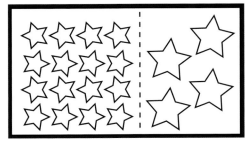

Placing Swags on 12" Block Quilt

1. Place quilt top on large table.

2. With hera marker or chalk and 6" x 24" ruler, draw guideline on Border 2" from inside seam on four sides. Guideline is marked in red.

3. Draw guideline from point of every Cornerstone to outside edge, including points on Cornerstones inside Side Triangles. See black lines on bottom and right sides.

4. For Corner Swags, mark two guidelines from Cornerstones.

2" guideline is marked in red. Guideline from every Cornerstone is marked in black.

Fusing Swags

1. Place pressing mat underneath top to press sections of Swag in place.

2. Place Swag on guidelines, and fuse in place with steam iron. There will be a ½" to 1" gap between Swags.

3. Continue placing Swags, moving pressing mat under Swags, and fusing in place with steam iron.

4. Continuously sew outside edges of Swags with straight stitch, blanket stitch, or blind hem stitch using invisible thread.

Placing Swags on 6" Block Quilt

1. With hera marker or chalk and 6" x 24" ruler, draw guideline on Border 1½" from inside seam on four sides. Guideline is marked in red.

2. Draw guideline from point of every outside Cornerstone to outside edge.

3. Two Swags are overlapped for corners.

4. Refer to Fusing Swags on left page.

1½" guideline is marked in red. Guideline from every Cornerstone is marked in grey.

Pressing and Sewing Stars

1. Center Stars on top of Swags.

2. Press in place for 8 – 10 seconds. Check edges to make sure they fused in place.

3. Finish outside raw edges with blanket stitch or straight stitch.

4. Turn to Finishing Your Quilt, page 226.

Sewing Straight Set Top and Ribbon Border

Squaring Your Blocks

1. Check that each block is a consistent size approximately 12½" or 6½" square. Your blocks may be consistently 12¼" or 6¼".

   For blocks larger than consistent size, sliver trim without trimming away any part of the ¼" seam allowance. Use a 12½" Square Up Ruler for 12" finished size blocks, and a 6½" Triangle Square Up Ruler for 6" finished size blocks. If necessary, resew a wider seam.

   For blocks smaller than consistent size, check seam widths and pressing. Unsew any wider seams and sew again with narrower seam.

2. Do not be concerned if there is a ¼" variance in block sizes. They can be stretched to size of other blocks.

Sewing Top Together

1. Cut Lattice to consistent size of block.
2. Lay out blocks, mixing colors and shapes. Place Lattice and Cornerstones between blocks.

Twenty 12" Blocks	Twenty 6" Blocks
4 x 5	4 x 5
(49) 3½" Lattice	(49) 4½" Lattice
(30) 3½" Cornerstones	(30) 2" Cornerstones

Twelve 12" Blocks	Twelve 6" Blocks
3 x 4	3 x 4
(31) 2½" Lattice	(31) 2" Lattice
(20) 5½" Cornerstones	(20) 2" Cornerstones

3. Assembly-line sew vertical rows together. Do not clip connecting threads.
4. Sew horizontal rows, pressing seams toward Lattice. Press top.

Sewing First Border

Strips are cut two different widths so Ribbon Border fits. You may need to make adjustments based on your seam allowance and pressing techniques.

1. Sew side strips into one long piece.

2. Measure sides, and cut two pieces the average length.

3. Pin and sew to sides.

4. Set seams with First Border on top, open, and press toward Border.

5. Sew top and bottom strips together into one long piece.

6. Measure top and bottom, and cut two pieces the average length.

7. Pin and sew to top and bottom.

8. Set seams with Border on top, open, and press toward Border.

Making Patches for Ribbon Border

For more detail, follow directions beginning on pages 164, substituting Ribbon Border measurements.

1. Draw diagonal lines on wrong side of Background squares for Little points.

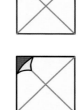

Twenty 12" Blocks	Twenty 6" Blocks
(19) 5½" squares	(13) 2" squares

Twelve 12" Blocks	Twelve 6" Blocks
(14) 2½" squares	(11) 4½" squares

2. Place right sides together to medium red squares for Little Points.

3. Sew ¼" from diagonal lines. See page 164. Cut apart on both drawn diagonal lines into four triangles.

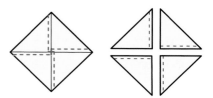

5. Press seams toward medium red.

6. Cut dark blue squares for Large Points in half on one diagonal.

Twenty 12" Blocks	Twenty 6" Blocks
(38) 5" squares	(26) 4" squares

Twelve 12" Blocks	Twelve 6" Blocks
(28) 5" squares	(22) 4" squares

7. Assembly-line sew triangles together.

8. Square with Fussy Cut Ruler.

12" Blocks	6" Blocks
4½" Fussy Cut Ruler	3½" Fussy Cut Ruler

Making Four Corner Patches

1. Draw diagonal line on wrong side of two Background squares.

12" Blocks	6" Blocks
(2) 5" squares	(2) 4" squares

2. Place right sides together to two medium red squares.

3. Sew ¼" seam from diagonal line.

4. Cut in half on diagonal line.

5. Set seam with red on top, open, and press toward red.

6. Square with Fussy Cut Ruler.

12" Blocks	6" Blocks
4½" Fussy Cut Ruler	3½" Fussy Cut Ruler

Sewing Ribbon Border Patches Together

1. Count out patches for one side at a time. Make four stacks.

Twenty 12" Blocks	Twenty 6" Blocks
Sides	Sides
(21) each	(14) each
Top and Bottom	Top and Bottom
(17) each	(12) each

Twelve 12" Blocks	Twelve 6" Blocks
Sides	Sides
(16) each	(12) each
Top and Bottom	Top and Bottom
(12) each	(10) each

Sew one side at a time.

2. Assembly-line sew one stack together at a time, locking seams.

3. Make two Sides, one Top, and one Bottom.

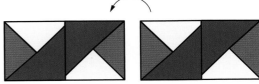

4. Press seams to one side.

Sewing Ribbon Border to Sides

1. Measure against long side of quilt top to see if they are the same size.

   If Ribbon Border is longer than sides, take in some seams. If Ribbon Border is too short, let out some seams. The Background strip can also be trimmed to fit.

2. Pin and sew to long sides of quilt.

3. Press just sewn seams toward First Border.

Sewing Ribbon Border to Top and Bottom

1. Sew Corner patch to each end.

3. Press seams to one side.

4. Measure against top and bottom of quilt top to see if they are the same size. Make seam adjustments if necessary.

5. Pin and sew to quilt.

6. Press just sewn seams toward First Border.

Finishing Top

1. Piece Second Border strips together.

2. Measure long sides, and cut two pieces the average length. Pin and sew to sides.

3. Set seams with Border on top, open, and press toward Border.

4. Measure top and bottom, and cut two pieces the average length. Pin and sew to top and bottom.

5. Set seams with Border on top, open, and press toward Border.

52" x 62"
Pieced and Quilted by Elisabeth Pfeiffer
Elisabeth customized her quilt by making 9" blocks,
and added a Ribbon Border to fit on an On Point Setting.

Finishing Your Quilt

Long Arm Quilting

Some quilters prefer to complete a top and send it to a long arm quilter.
Follow these instructions if long arm quilting is your choice.

1. Clip loose threads. Make sure there are no loose or unsewn seams. Have top free of embellishments.

2. Press top and have it as wrinkle-free as possible. This applies to the backing fabric also.

3. The side measurements should be the same, and the top and bottom measurements should also be the same.

4. The backing fabric should be 4-6" longer and wider than the quilt top measurements. For example, if the quilt top is 90" x 108", then the backing should be 94" x 112" minimum.

5. The batting should be no less than 6" longer and wider than the pieced top measurements.

6. Do not pin the three layers together.

Some long arm quilters charge hourly prices depending on the density of the design, thread requests, and other factors. Others base the charge on the square inch size of the quilt. Your local quilt shop can often provide the names of local long arm quilters if you need help locating one.

88" x 108"
Pieced by Teresa Varnes
Quilted by Cindee Ferris

Machine Quilting on a Conventional Sewing Machine

Layering Your Quilt

Follow these steps if you plan to quilt on a conventional sewing machine.

1. If necessary, piece Backing approximately 4"-6" larger than finished top.

2. Spread out Backing on a large table or floor area, right side down. Clamp fabric to edge of table with quilt clips, or tape Backing to the floor. Do not stretch Backing.

3. Layer Batting on Backing, also 4"-6" larger than finished top. Pat flat.

4. With right side up, center quilt on Batting and Backing. Smooth until all layers are flat. Clamp or tape outside edges.

Safety Pinning

1. Place pin covers on 1" safety pins with needle nose pliers.

2. Pin away from where you plan to quilt. Catch tip of pin in grooves on pinning tool, and close pins.

3. Safety pin through all layers three to five inches apart.

4. Use pinning tool to open pins when removing them. Store pins opened.

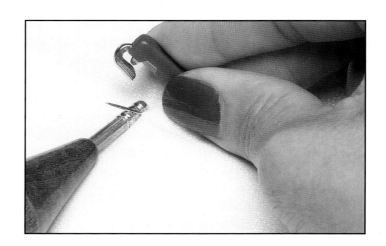

"Stitch in the Ditch" along Lattice and Borders

1. Thread your machine with matching thread or invisible thread. If you use invisible thread, loosen your top tension. Match the bobbin thread to the Backing.

2. Attach your walking foot, and lengthen the stitch to 8 to 10 stitches per inch or 3.5 on computerized machines.

3. Tightly roll quilt from one long side to Lattice. Place hands on quilt in triangular shape, and spread seams open. Stitch in the ditch along seam lines and anchor blocks and border.

4. Roll quilt in opposite direction, and stitch in the ditch along seam lines.

"Stitch in the Ditch" around Blocks

1. With your walking foot, stitch in the ditch on seam lines around block.

2. If desired, quilt ¼" away from seams.

3. You can also stitch in the ditch with a darning foot so that you don't need to constantly pivot and turn a large heavy quilt as you do with a walking foot.

Marking for Free Motion Quilting

1. Select an appropriate stencil.

2. Center on area to be quilted, and trace lines with disappearing marker. An alternative method is lightly spraying fabric with water, and blue pouncing powder into lines of stencil.

Quilting with Darning Foot

1. Attach darning foot to sewing machine. Drop feed dogs or cover feed dogs with a plate. No stitch length is required as you control the length by your sewing speed. Use a fine needle and regular thread in the top and regular thread to match the Backing in the bobbin. Use needle down position.

2. Place hands flat around marked design. Bring bobbin thread up on line.

3. Lock stitch and clip thread tails. Free motion stitch **on marked lines**. Keep top of block at top. Sew sideways and back and forth without turning quilt.

4. Stipple Background area by stitching a few stitches in one direction. Curve around and stitch back toward the beginning, making a loop. Continue making loops until Background area is filled.

5. Lock stitches and cut threads.

Straight Cut Binding

These instructions show how to make a one-fabric Binding. If desired, make a Scrappy Binding by cutting leftover fabric into 3" wide strips by any length and piece them together to fit around outside edge of quilt top. Follow these instructions for either one.

1. Square off selvage edges, and sew 3" Binding strips together lengthwise. Fold and press in half with wrong sides together.

2. Place walking foot attachment on sewing machine and regular thread on top and in bobbin to match Binding.

3. Line up raw edges of folded Binding with raw edges of quilt in middle of one side. Begin stitching 4" from end of Binding. Sew with 10 stitches per inch, or 3.0 to 3.5. Sew approximately ⅜" from edge, or width of walking foot.

4. Place pin ⅜" from corner.

5. At corner, stop stitching by pin ⅜" in from edge with needle in fabric. Remove pin. Raise presser foot and turn quilt toward corner.

6. Put presser foot down. Stitch diagonally off edge of Binding.

7. Raise foot, and pull quilt forward slightly.

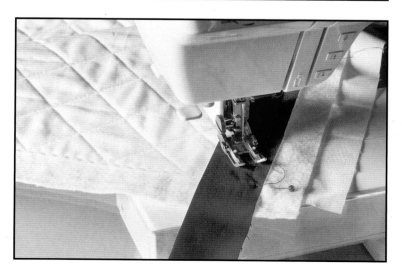

8. Turn quilt to next side.

9. Fold Binding strip straight up on diagonal. Fingerpress diagonal fold.

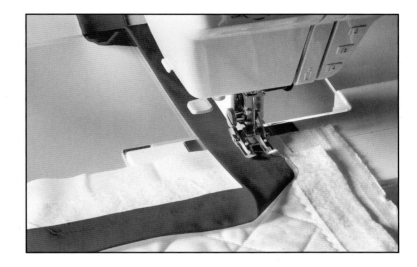

10. Fold Binding strip straight down with diagonal fold underneath. Line up top of fold with raw edge of Binding underneath.

11. Begin sewing from edge.

12. Continue stitching and mitering corners around outside of quilt.

13. Stop stitching 4" from where ends will overlap.

14. Line up two ends of Binding. Trim excess with ½" overlap.

15. Open out folded ends and pin right sides together. Sew a ¼" seam. Press seam open.

16. Continue stitching Binding in place.

17. Trim Batting and Backing up to ⅛" from raw edges of Binding.

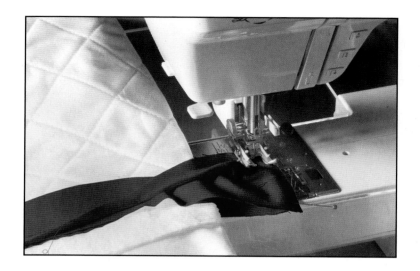

18. Fold back Binding.

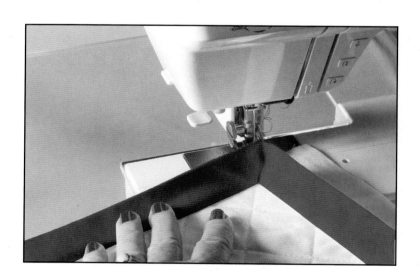

19. Pull Binding to back side of quilt. Pin in place so that folded edge on Binding covers stitching line. Tuck in excess fabric at each miter on diagonal.

20. From right side, "stitch in the ditch" using invisible or matching thread on front side, and bobbin thread to match Binding on back side. Catch folded edge of Binding on the back side with stitching.

Optional: Hand stitch Binding in place.

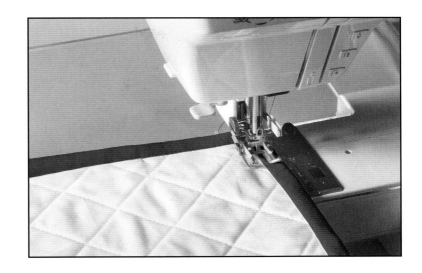

21. Hand stitch miter.

22. Sew identification label on Back.

- name of maker
- place where quilt was made
- year
- name of quilt
- any other pertinent information.

USO Show

In keeping with the Victory Quilts theme, an end of the year USO Show was performed with talent from Quilt in a Day staff. Block Party ladies had the opportunity to show off their finished quilts.

Staff Cindi Russell, Andrew Lawandus, and Becky Turner lip sinc Boggie Woogie Bugle Boy, while the "troops" listen.

Orion Burns dancing as a young Bob Hope

Eleanor Burns dancing the Victory Polka with her sister, Patricia Knoechel

Chris Levine

Anne Tracy

Sally Murray

Laura Weston

Two "Rosies", Diane Knight and Eleanor Burns

Linda Holt and Marcia Woolf

Diane's quilt is a combination of two blocks: Broken Sugar Bowl and Stars and Stripes.

Heidi McFadden and Friends

Heidi, a Navy reservist, choose desert colored batiks in honor of Marines that fought in the South Pacific during World War II.

Macy Silveria in her Fala Nighty

Sue Bouchard and Eleanor Burns share a special quilt by vogies@vogies.com

Jeane Stellmack

Charmaine Wade

Hinde Socol

Brenda Witt with her father's picture

Elizabeth Pfeiffer

6" Block Templates

12" Block Templates included in Back Pocket

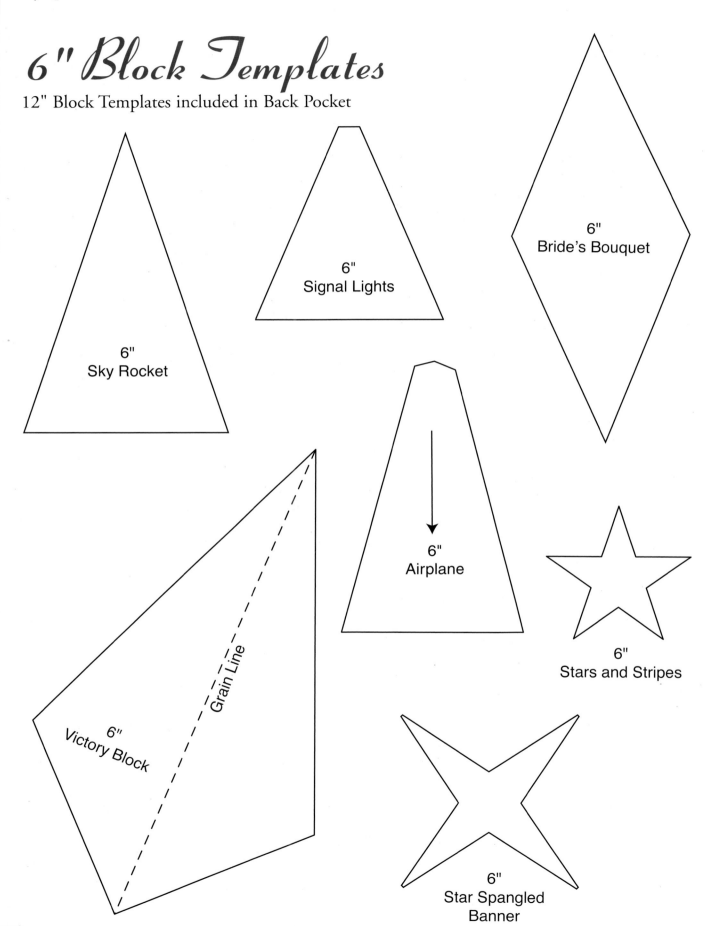

6"
Sky Rocket

6"
Signal Lights

6"
Bride's Bouquet

6"
Airplane

6"
Victory Block

Grain Line

6"
Stars and Stripes

6"
Star Spangled
Banner

"Bad Dog" Quilt

Elizabeth Peay found these 1930's quilt blocks, and sewed them together. When Elizabeth showed the completed quilt to her husband, he immediately noticed one block unintentionally turned wrong, and said "Bad dog!"

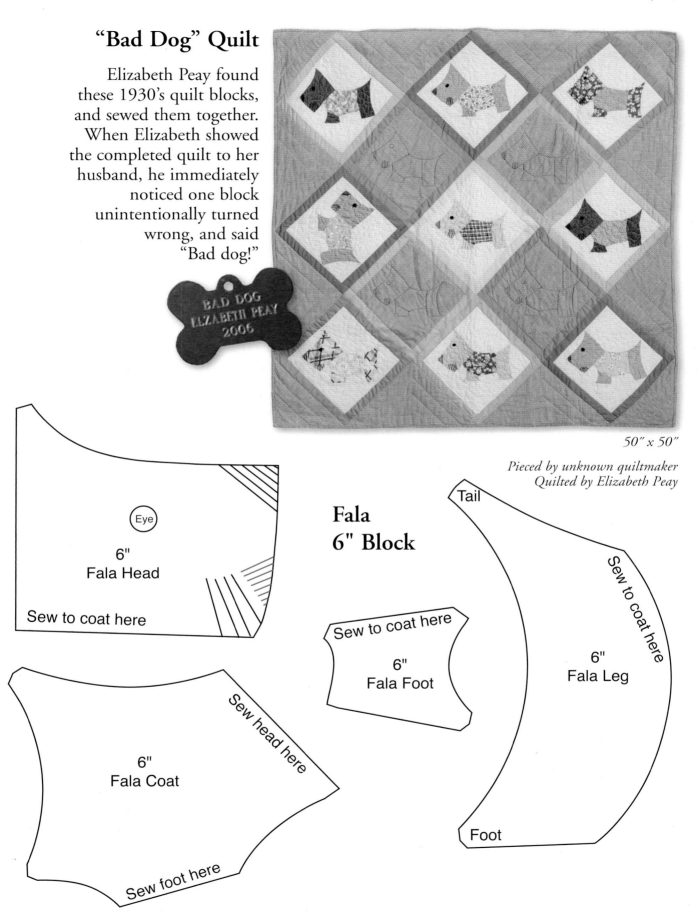

50" x 50"

Pieced by unknown quiltmaker
Quilted by Elizabeth Peay

Fala
6" Block

Eye

6"
Fala Head

Sew to coat here

6"
Fala Coat

Sew head here

Sew foot here

Sew to coat here

6"
Fala Foot

Tail

Sew to coat here

6"
Fala Leg

Foot

Index

Wave a Flag for these Gals

Piecers

2007 Block Party
Sue Bouchard
Kari Gjerde
Linda Holt
Patricia Knoechel

Sally Murray
Elizabeth Peay
Anne Tracy
Amber Varnes
Teresa Varnes

Long Arm Quilters

Cindee Ferris
Judy Jackson
Janna Mitchell
Amie Potter
Carol Selepec

Additional Reading

Passing on the Comfort, *The War, the Quilts, and the Women Who Made a Difference*
by An Keuning-Tichelaar and Lynn Kaplanian-Buller
Published by Good Books, 2005

Rosie the Riveter, *Women Working on the Home Front in World War II*
by Penny Coleman
Published by Crown Publishers, Inc., 1995

"We Pulled Together ...and Won!", *Personal Memories of the World War II Years...*
Published by Roy J. Reiman, Reminisce Books, 1993

Order Information

Quilt in a Day offers Patriotic Fabric Kits, Printed Swag and Stars Interfacing, Mini Geese Rulers, and Fussy Cut Rulers to help you complete your Victory Quilt. Call us or check our website for current information.

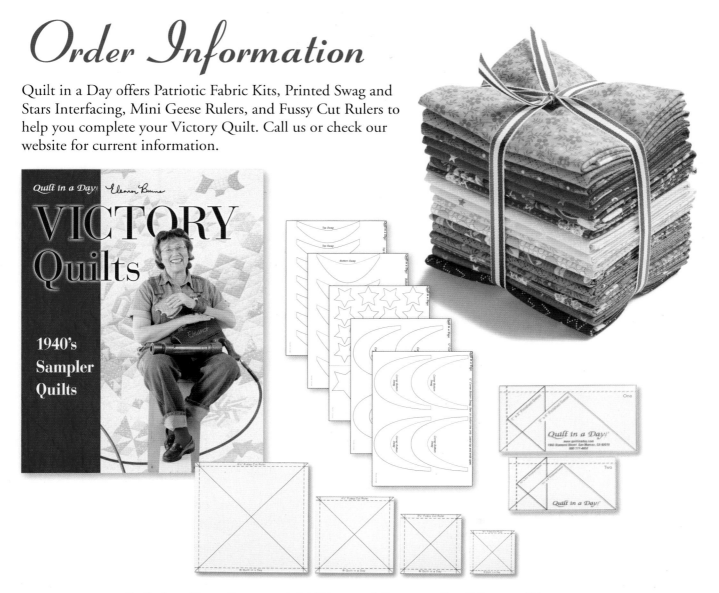

Quilt in a Day®, Inc. • 1955 Diamond Street • San Marcos, CA 92078
800 777-4852 • Fax: 760 591-4424 • www.quiltinaday.com

With scrap bag in hand, Linda Holt carefully planned and executed her Sampler. She used a variety of prints and tones to give her quilt a vintage look. Her prominent use of bright yellow just sets her quilt off perfectly. She finished her 12" blocks on-point and added a blue and green swag to frame her blocks. Judy Jackson did a great job with the machine quilting.

A Touch of Spring

With light hearted pastels and fussy cut flowers, my sister Patricia Knoechel's quilt resembles a spring garden of flowers. Her 6" blocks are set straight with lattice and cornerstones. She repeated a few favorite blocks and added a pieced pastel blue ribbon border. This quilt is ready for baby!